THE POST

Alan James

B. T. BATSFORD LTD   London

First published 1970
© Alan James, 1970

Filmset by Keyspools Ltd, Golborne, Lancs.

Printed in Great Britain by Billing & Sons Ltd, Guildford, Surrey
for the Publishers
B. T. Batsford Ltd, 4 Fitzhardinge Street, London W1

7134 1764 1

Contents

Acknowledgment

Figs. 17, 24, 26, 30, 32, 34, 35, 42, 48 and 59 were photographed from items in the author's collection by R. P. N. Rees. The author and publisher would also like to thank the following for permission to reproduce the illustrations as listed: Central Press Photos Ltd. for frontispiece; Ministry of Public Buildings and Works for fig. 52; National Postal Museum, Reginald M. Phillips Collection, for figs. 21, 31 and 39; The Post Office for figs. 1, 2, 4–7, 9, 10, 12–16, 19, 22, 25, 28, 36, 38, 40, 41, 43–47, 49–51, 53–58 and 60–62; Raphael Tuck & Sons Ltd. for fig. 37.

The Illustrations

H.M. the Queen opens the extended National Postal Museum in London in February 1969. The National Postal Museum contains a rare collection of postal history and British stamps as well as stamps from all over the world. Its exhibits are on view to the public and visits are recommended highly. The Museum is situated in King Edward Street close to St Paul's Underground. Admission free.

Introduction

The word Post has a variety of meanings. Its use in earlier times was often indiscriminate and it was used commonly with a wider range of meanings than it is today. Post could refer to the postal system in general, to the carrier of letters, to the person in charge of a relay station and perhaps even to the horse. The word also meant a single dispatch of letters, or to travel with haste. It was used to describe the bag in which letters were carried, and messengers could travel post by hiring horses and guides at a fixed charge per mile from the postmasters at the stages.

This book tells the story of one of the most important social developments of all – the sending of letters, the real revolution in which did not occur until 1840. Before any of the forms of mass media we take for granted each day in our lives had even been introduced, the letter was of greater value still. It provided a form of message that was private, that usually arrived safely, that was a permanent record for sentiment or reference and that awaited the convenience of the recipient. Letters had to be sent by a postal system of some kind, either private or public, and it is the development of the complex machinery of the Post that this book sets out to trace. As Henry Cole, one of the mid-nineteenth-century postal reformers, ardently believed:

All the progress of mankind is helped on by freedom of thought expressed in writing. The progress of religion, morals, health, science, education, arts, manufactures, commerce and international peace, are all advanced by correspondence which is next to nothing without the Post Office.

To My Mother and Father

1 Early Posts

Letters were written and sent in early times, but the numbers of people who could read and write were few, and there was no postal service as we know it today. The organisation of a post, if such existed, was meant for the king only. Other people who wanted to send letters had to find their own means of doing so. Kings employed letter-carriers to deliver their messages and decrees to distant parts of their kingdoms. The messengers of King Hezekiah, mentioned in the Old Testament, ran from city to city throughout the land delivering the king's word. 'So the posts went with the letters from the king and his princes throughout all Israel and Judah, according to the commandment of the king,' (II *Chronicles* 30,6).

Herodotus, the Greek historian, relates that after Xerxes, king of Persia, and lord of an empire stretching from India to Ethiopia, had invaded Greece he sent messengers back to Persia with news of his victory at the Battle of Salamis (480 B.C.). In doing so he used an established messenger service. Horses and men were positioned along the main routes, at intervals of a day's journey, and the message was passed 'from hand to hand along the whole line, like the light in a torch race'. The postal service of Xerxes, more unfamiliarly known as King Ahasuerus, is also mentioned in the Bible:

> In the name of King Ahasuerus was it written, and it was sealed with the king's ring. And letters were sent by posts into all the king's provinces . . . the posts went forth in haste by the king's commandment (*Esther* 3).

> And he wrote in the name of King Ahasuerus, and sealed it with the king's ring, and sent letters by posts on horseback, riding on swift steeds [or 'swift steeds, mules and young dromedaries'] that were used in the king's service, bred in the stud (*Esther* 8).

Despite the great and difficult distances involved, the messages of these early potentates were delivered with all speed and reliability. Cyrus the Great had introduced a postal service to Persia in the mid sixth century B.C., and Herodotus praised these alien messengers when he wrote: 'Neither rain nor sun nor heat nor gloom of night stays these couriers from their appointed rounds.' A century later, the Persian system was probably just as well-maintained, judging from Xenophon's remark that the Persian king's messages travelled more quickly than cranes in flight.

The responsibilities and hazards of these early postmen were tremendous.

They were expected to travel at all speed with important matters of state; frequently they had to cross frontiers and travel amongst hostile foreigners. A piece of Egyptian clay, dated to 2300 B.C., thus describes a messenger's existence: 'Before departing, he maketh over his fortune to his children for fear of the Asiatics and the wild animals. . . . Scarce hath he returned home but he must set forth again.'

Greek city states had to cope with far smaller distances than the Persians. The Greeks communicated, state with state, by the use of messengers who ran. These were the famous *hemeradromoi* ('runners the day through'), described by a contemporary: 'They are young men but recently out of their childhood . . . nought take they with them save bow and arrow, spear and sling; for these things are found to be of great service to them on their course.'

The heroism of these runners has passed into legend, the most famous case being the runner who fell dead at the Acropolis in Athens after bringing news of the victory at Marathon – a run commemorated in the Marathon in the modern Olympic Games. Another, Pheidippides, is thought to have run 150 miles, from Athens to Sparta, in two days, with news of the Persian invasion.

The Romans too had extensive postal arrangements to link their far-flung territories. Travel improved on the Roman roads, and the Romans requisitioned carts, horses and even vessels to assist in the speedy transmission of the mail – though no really substantial increases in postal speeds occurred until the railways were used to carry mail in the nineteenth century. Throughout the Roman Empire a post was set up called the *cursus publicus,* and letters were carried on horseback via a system of relay stations where fresh teams were always held in readiness. The Romans also developed a variety of parcel posts.

Early letters were written on papyrus (a material rather like paper, made from river reed) with a reed pen, or in Roman times on tablets. These tablets were made of wood or ivory, covered with wax, and the words were written on the wax with a stylus. Parchment did not become common until the Roman Empire began to disintegrate and, of course, paper was not used widely until the close of the Middle Ages.

The Sumerians of Mesopotamia have left clay tablets at least 5,000 years old, written on in cuneiform (a wedge-shaped script). The Egyptians wrote on papyrus and on clay tablets. Though there are many Egyptian tablets in existence, invaluable from a general historical viewpoint, often they are of little help to the postal historian, for the majority of them do not consist of personal letters. Yet many letters have survived. Pharaoh Akhenaten kept a storehouse of official tablets at Amarna, which were discovered towards the end of the nineteenth century. These tablets were letters sent by foreign kings to Egypt and were written in Babylonian cuneiform script, which was also used in Palestine and Syria.

Assurbanipol of Assyria collected more than 20,000 clay tablets into a library, including tablets of prayers, hymns and legends, and facts about the planets, science, medicine, mathematics; there were even clay dictionaries.

The Arabs began a postal service, and in the seventh century there were six postal routes from Baghdad and along them there were almost 1,000 relay stations placed about a day's journey apart, which was about a dozen miles or so. Horse posts were used to carry the most urgent messages, while foot messengers or messengers on camels provided a more leisurely service.

One rather clever way of sending messages had been used since early times, in containers strapped to the legs of pigeons. Pigeons were used for this purpose by the Greeks, the Romans, the Chinese and the Arabs, and they were made an important means of communication in Egypt in the Middle Ages by the Mamelukes, who built pigeon lofts every few miles along important routes. Racing pigeons were used to carry the most important messages and blue pigeons to carry ordinary letters. Of course, the safe arrival of a letter could not be guaranteed, and for this reason each one of real importance would be sent at least twice, by different pigeons, in the hope that one of them would escape hawks and get the message through.

Detailed information about the earliest posts is slight, both because of the time gap and because services were confined to king and state, and did not extend to private citizens. The same is true of Britain until the profound changes in the postal system inaugurated by the Tudors.

In Britain in the Middle Ages various attempts were made to unite the kingdom with a postal service, but most of these attempts were short-lived affairs. Some of them can be noted briefly here. Henry I (1100–1135) had carriers of letters, and Edward I (1272–1307) organised stages where horses were stabled for the carriers. It was Henry IV (1399–1413) who began the postboy system, and often the stages where fresh mounts were to be obtained were inns, not always on the roads. Frequently the postboys found it quicker to leave the roads, such as they were, and to travel through private land. They were messengers of the crown, and their right to do this, though criticised, had to be tolerated. Edward IV (1461–1483) set up a temporary post to the north in 1481, when England was at war with Scotland. There were relay posts at 20-mile intervals along the road, but this system lapsed after the war ended.

Apart from royal messages, the only kind to be sent by the systems already noted, other people desired to send letters. As yet, their numbers were not large by later standards but, even so, the total was quite considerable. Universities, many of which had foreign students, kept up a steady flow of correspondence; monasteries and other religious foundations sent letters from one institution to another; lawyers and the judicial world as a whole needed to correspond; merchants were another group whose businesses often relied on a flow of information, frequently from abroad. European traders in Britain developed a regular system of sending letters by means of their own ships, known to the British as the Strangers' Post. Later, similar arrangements were developed by British traders. Even the royal mail was sometimes carried by any means that were available. The records of the Privy Council show, for example, that in 1430 £10 was paid to a couple of friars 'who brought letters from the town of Paris and the King's Council there'.

If the royal post was occasionally dependent on chance carriers, how much more so was the ordinary literate person. Ordinary people must often have written letters and sent them off in the vague hope that they might reach their destinations. A wealthy person might have a servant to deliver his letters, but others had to rely on help from friends setting off on journeys or even on the goodwill of strangers.

It was all too easy to steal from letters which were simply large sheets of paper folded several times and sealed on the back with wax. If they contained anything, this might be apparent at once. Often these letters were addressed in ways which make one wonder that so many of them actually seemed to arrive. Letters have survived written by a Norfolk family, the Pastons, throughout much of the fifteenth century, and one, for example, was addressed 'To Edmond Paston of Cliffordes Inn, in London, be this letter take'.

By the beginning of the sixteenth century there were many private carriers of ordinary letters; but these were by no means encouraged by monarchs such as Elizabeth I, who suspected messages sent by individuals – sometimes with just cause.

Henry VIII (1509–1547) appointed Brian Tuke as the first Master of the Posts. The old relay systems were brought into use again, with stages at inns 10 or 15 miles apart. If a royal messenger carried a letter himself, he was shown the route to follow by a postboy, who returned when the next stage was reached. Other official letters were carried from stage to stage by different messengers. There were always posts in operation in the sixteenth century on important routes, such as from London to Dover and so to the Continent, and also the road to Scotland. Temporary routes would be set up as the occasion demanded. If the navy was at Portsmouth, then a post might be set up there. Also 'wherever the king is, posts are laid from London to his Grace'.

At first, such local officials as constables and bailiffs were probably in charge of providing sufficient horses and men for each post. Later, no doubt as a result of the increase in posts, and the heavier work involved, the responsibility for ensuring that post stages were maintained appears to have passed to the hostelries. The innkeepers hung out a sign indicating a post horn. In a sense, the inns were the first post offices and the innkeepers the first postmasters.

Under Elizabeth I (1558–1603) it became an offence to carry letters abroad for anyone not on the staff of the Master of the Posts. Certainly, letters sent abroad offered ample opportunity for plotting and spying against the crown, and if this appears a little melodramatic it must be remembered that the events of the Armada and the execution of Mary Stuart had taken place only a few years before. During her imprisonment, Mary Stuart carried on an extensive correspondence with the ambassador from Spain. This she doubtless believed to be secret, but in fact it was known to Walsingham, Secretary of State to Elizabeth,

who read the letters (both incoming and outgoing) before allowing them to be sent. The means Mary used to communicate were as numerous as they were ingenious. Messages were written on particular pages in books and hidden inside the heels of shoes. Letters which she received from abroad arrived at her prison inside beer kegs, wrapped in a waterproof covering. Some of her letters sent out of prison were placed inside the empty kegs. But Walsingham, fearing plots, read them all.

Elizabeth's enactment of 1591 was impossible to enforce, and merchants travelling overseas continued as before to carry letters for a fee. By this time there were unofficial letter-carriers for inland mail, but under Thomas Randolph, Master of the Queen's Posts, letters from private individuals were accepted and carried in the official bag, though priority was given to delivering official letters. The speeds of travelling did not seem to improve much in the sixteenth century. On the north route, for instance – a busy one from London into Scotland – the stage from Durham to Newcastle, a distance of 14 miles, took 16 hours. The

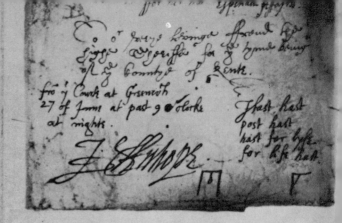

2 Letter addressed to the Sheriff of Kent in the reign of Elizabeth I. Notice the gallows drawn in the bottom right-hand corner. Perhaps these were an indication of the business of the letter or a warning to the postal messenger not to tarry.

Dover route, immortalised by Chaucer in *The Canterbury Tales,* was another busy one, and the markings on a letter to Cecil, Elizabeth's minister, are of interest:

> For Her Majesty's especial affairs. Hast, Hast, Hast, Hast, Post Hast, Hast for Life. June 22 at Sandwich at seven of the clock in the afternoon. Canterbury past nine at night. Sittingbourne at past twelve at night. Rochester the 23 at one in the morning. Dartford the 23 four in the morning.

Speeds of between five and seven miles an hour were required officially from post-boys, though it is clear that actual speeds were often a good deal less. If need be, however, it was possible to convey a message very quickly from one part of the country to the other. Such was the case when, on the death of Elizabeth in 1603, Sir Robert Carey rode from London to Edinburgh to carry the news to James VI of Scotland. Carey set out from London after nine on the morning of 25 March, arrived at Doncaster the same evening, and completed the last part of the journey of just over 400 miles late on the 27th, having travelled at an average speed of about seven miles an hour – a creditable performance by any standards.

FURTHER READING
H. Robinson, *The British Post Office*

2 Postal Changes, 1600–1784

Early in the seventeenth century, James I issued a proclamation similar to that of Elizabeth prohibiting private letter-carriers, but his attempt to keep the monopoly for the crown was far from successful. Lord Stanhope was official Master of the Posts at this time, his patent giving him responsibility for inland letters as well as those sent abroad. However, Matthew de Quester, a Flemish merchant who lived in England, gradually came to be in effective charge of the foreign posts. De Quester's appointment as Postmaster of England for Foreign Parts in 1619 led to a dispute with Stanhope. As a result, de Quester retained his title, but in 1632 foreign letters were put under the control of Frizell and Thomas Witherings, and Witherings soon established the first regular postal service by boat across the English Channel. Delays in sailing had been frequent, as the boatmen often did not leave as soon as they received the bag of letters. Witherings hired a boatman at Dover who guaranteed to sail immediately the mail arrived from London. Then the boatman waited at Calais for the letters to come from Antwerp. Witherings also helped to improve the inland mails. In 1635 under Charles I the royal postal system was opened to the public, who paid postage based on a fixed scale of charges.

Witherings soon had in operation a working system along the six principal post roads of England, from London to Dover, Yarmouth, Edinburgh, Chester, Bristol and Plymouth. The unsettled political climate of the times was against any lasting improvement in the postal service. In an attempt to prevent political intrigue, the only letters to be carried from 1637 were those travelling on royal or governmental business. The Post Office remained in a confused state during the Civil War, as different groups attempted to gain its control.

The Post Office Act of 1660 established one General Post Office for the country and one Postmaster General, operating a postal system open to all. A letter of one sheet was to be carried for 80 miles for 2d. in England. Places of some size that were not on the main post roads were to have 'constant posts for the carriage of letters to all places, though they lie out of the post roads'. Thus, Kendal, Lincoln and Grimsby, for instance, became entitled to a weekly post. The government allowed the position of Postmaster General to be purchased by the highest bidder, who then had to make the postal service pay in order to recoup himself for the initial expense. Any extra postal income was kept by the Postmaster General as his profit on the initial payment, which was often very large. Henry Bishop was appointed Postmaster General in 1660 at a yearly rental of £21,500. Bishop is famed for his invention of the Bishop mark – the first kind of postmark – which consisted of a small circle divided with a bar across the middle. In the upper

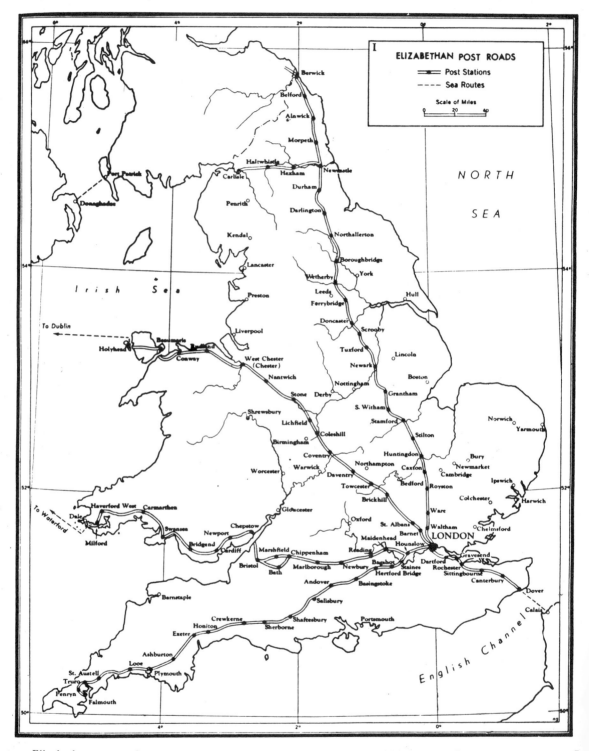

3 Elizabethan post roads.

half of the circle were letters standing for the month (NO meant November, SE meant September) and in the lower half the day of the month on which the letter was posted. The year was not indicated, and so it was not possible to tell in which year a letter was posted unless, of course, the correspondent wrote the full date on the letter himself. Complaints from the public about slow delivery are certainly not of modern origin, and the Bishop mark was introduced to help keep a check on letters in the post: 'A stamp is invented that is putt upon every letter shewing the day of the moneth that every letter comes to the office, so that no Letter Carryer may dare to detayne a letter from post to post, which before was usual.'

At this time the staff of the Post Office in London was under 50. In 1665 there were 45 employed on the Post Office staff in London, of whom 30 died in the Plague of that year. There were five receiving houses in London where the public could hand in their letters, which were then sent to the General Letter Office. During the Great Plague letters were aired over vinegar in a vain attempt to prevent the spread of disease but, as one postal official recorded, the 'Post Office is so fumed morning and night that they can hardly see each other. Had the contagion been catching by letters they had been dead long ago.' London was hit by a second disaster in the following year, when the Great Fire swept over the city. The Post Office, which was then near the river, was in the path of the destruction, and temporary arrangements had to be made to house it elsewhere. Later the Post Office was rehoused in Bishopsgate, and in 1678 it was transferred to Lombard Street, where it remained until it was moved to St Martin's le Grand in the nineteenth century.

Many mail routes were still very slow. A letter from London to Dublin took about six days to arrive, depending much on wind and weather. Letters from London to Bristol were sent in 30 hours if everyone along the route worked to schedule, which was not always the case:

To Mr Sadler, Postmaster of Marlborough. I can no longer endure your shameful neglect of the mails. I have grievous complaints from Bristol of the prejudice they receive thereby; and find that it is 7, 8, 9 or 10 hours commonly betwixt you and Chippenham, which is but 15 miles, and ought to be performed in 3 hours.

One of the most curious, as well as successful, of the private-venture experiments of the seventeenth century was the London Penny Post established by William Dockwra, a merchant, in 1680. A proper postal service for London was certainly needed: it was often easier to send letters to the far ends of the country than from one part of the capital to another. The detailed organisation worked out for Dockwra's plan was immense. London was divided into districts, each with an office. The head office of the system was at Dockwra's house in Lyme Street. Each district office was a sorting office. Many hundreds of receiving houses were opened, placards hanging outside them reading 'Penny Post letters taken in here'. Dockwra's messengers collected letters and parcels from these receiving houses each hour, and took them to the sorting office of the district. When letters had been sorted for delivery they were sent on to their destinations almost at once. In the more remote parts of urban London, there were often about six deliveries of letters to homes each day. But the business areas of London fared even better: they had about 12 deliveries each day! Dockwra charged a standard rate of a penny for each letter or parcel under a pound in weight. Letters that were destined for the more remote parts of the area which Dockwra covered had to pay an extra penny to be delivered. Of course, Londoners who wanted to send letters out of the capital had to use the General Post, but Dockwra's receiving houses were so numerous that many people delivered their non-London letters there, paying a penny for the convenience of doing so; they were then sent on by Dockwra's staff to the General Letter Office and from there they left London. As most people did not pay the postage on letters sent through the General Post until the letters were delivered at the door, Dockwra provided a useful service.

On the letters he carried he used handstamps, which showed where the letter had been received in the first place and also the day and time of day when the letter was handed in at the receiving house. Dockwra's Penny Post was paying its way well, but after two years he was fined and the government took over his service. In fact, it was amazing that he was allowed to go on as long as he did. Dockwra had defended his Penny Post by insisting that it did not overlap with the

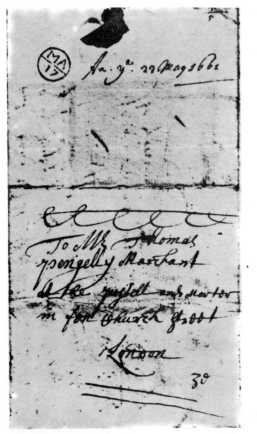

4 An early Bishop Mark on a letter dated 17 May 1661. The Bishop Mark, invented by the Postmaster-General, Henry Bishop, was circular and showed the month and day of the month the letter was received by the Post Office. This handstamp did not indicate the year of posting.

5 A postboy in the latter part of the seventeenth century. Letters were carried by footposts and by postboys until the introduction of the mail coach in the last years of the eighteenth century, and much later in some places.

Mail Routes
and
Post Towns
organised by
Thos. Witherings
1635–51

6   Map of Thomas Witherings' postal system in the seventeenth century.

services provided by the General Post. Towns and villages near London that were included within the area of the Penny Post were all 'within less distance than the nearest post stages . . . where the General Post Office had never settled any accommodation'. His assertion was truthful enough, a fact obviously realised by the government, who seemed to be glad to take over the responsibility for such a worthwhile and useful service. Much later, Dockwra applied for compensation for his work in founding the Penny Post. In 1696, having already received a grant of £500 a year for seven years, he was appointed Comptroller of the Penny Post. He did not long remain in that position. Both officers and messengers complained – with what justification we cannot be sure – of his behaviour 'as he was irregular, vexatious and troublesome, and not fit to be any longer borne with'. He was accused of refusing to accept heavy parcels and of detaining and even opening letters. He lost office in 1700.

There were three separate postal departments in London and three sets of letter-carriers. The Inland Office dealt with all letters for Britain, the Foreign (Letter) Office with foreign letters and packets, and the Penny Post Office with all local letters for London and its environs. Letters were sent constantly from one department to another in the London office. Three letters posted in Edinburgh to Paris, Bristol and Chelsea would be sent to the Inland Office, and then the letters for Chelsea and Paris would be transferred to the Penny Post Office and the Foreign Office respectively. The Inland Office was divided into six sections, one for each of the main roads – the Western, Bristol, Chester, North, Yarmouth and Kent roads. Letters were posted as well as called for at the General Post Office, where there were three windowmen on duty. Another clerk sorted letters alphabetically so that callers could collect their mail quickly.

It was nearly a century after the Post Office had taken over Dockwra's service before the next legal Penny Post was established, this time in 1773. Another illegal scheme was begun in London in 1709 by Charles Povey, who set up a halfpenny post. He had several receiving houses, and his collectors also travelled round the streets ringing a bell to let people know they were passing. Even though Povey's charge was less than that of the official Penny Post in London, and covered rather a different area, it was, nevertheless, an infringement of the established official service and was bound to be suppressed. By December, a warning was issued in no uncertain terms:

Whereas Charles Povey and divers Traders and Shop Keepers in and about the Cities of London and Westminster, Borough of Southwick and parts adjacent,.and several Persons ringing Bells about the Streets of the said Cities and Borough, have set up, imploy'd and for some time continued a Foot Post for Collecting and Delivering Letters within the said Cities and Borough, and Parts adjoining, for Hire under the Name of the Halfpenny Carriage. . . . Her Majesty's Postmaster General has Therefore directed Informations in Her Majesty's Court of Exchequer to be exhibited against the said Charles Povey,

7 Ralph Allen, Postmaster of Bath, who improved and extended the cross posts throughout the country and organised them into a working system.

and several Shop Keepers and Ringers of Bells, for Recovery against every one of them £100 for such setting up, and for every week's continuance thereof; and also £5 for every Offence in Collecting and Delivering of Letters for Hire as aforesaid, contrary to the Statute for erecting and establishing a Post Office.

Though Povey's halfpenny post lasted for about seven months only, one feature of it endured much longer. The Post Office began to use bellmen to collect letters in the streets, and these travelling post-boxes were continued until as late as 1846 in London.

The Post Office Act of 1711 was in part the result of Povey's experiment, as well as being an attempt to make the Post Office pay a share in the financial needs of the country. Yet, even after increased charges, losses were frequent. A single letter was carried in England and Wales for 3d. up to 80 miles. Foreign rates also increased: it now cost 10d. to send a letter from London to France, although in 1660 the charge had been only 4d. for a letter to Calais or Boulogne. A single letter to New York already cost one shilling.

Mails did not leave London every weekday evening until the second half of the eighteenth century. Before that time, they set out from London on Tuesday, Thursday and Saturday evenings, though on the other evenings letters were sent across Kent. Great inconvenience was suffered by people not living directly on a post road. The population had been growing steadily, yet places such as York, Lincoln, Hull, Derby, Leeds and Sheffield were not sited on post roads originally. Quick communication between places on different post routes was also a problem. A letter sent from Chester to Bristol, for example, had to go first to London to be re-routed along the Bristol road. Letters were charged according to distance travelled, and so roundabout routes resulted in greatly increased costs. A letter sent from York to Manchester by a direct route would have covered less than 70 miles. In fact, such a letter had to travel first to London and then north again to Manchester – a distance of close on 400 miles! What was needed was a comprehensive system of cross-posts which connected places on different post roads by the shortest routes possible. The post roads, radiating from London, served as spokes of a wheel, but these spokes needed to be joined together to create an intricate web of routes throughout the country. Some branch routes and cross-posts had been introduced in the seventeenth century, but a detailed system was not worked out until Ralph Allen turned his attention to the problem in the eighteenth century.

Ralph Allen was postmaster at Bath, and in 1720 he was granted the responsibility for cross-letters and by-letters. Cross-posts were unofficial routes linking places on different post roads. By-posts carried letters that did not have to pass through London. Allen made these posts pay well and earned much from his postal successes. Before Allen began his work, there were several cross-posts, one of which – that between Exeter and Bristol – opened in 1696 and reduced the postal charge from 6d. to 2d. Allen had to deal with much corruption in the postal service. One Post Office official discovered that there was a building at Plymouth where postboys met to exchange letters for which they had taken payment which they kept for themselves and, of course, they kept quiet about carrying these extra letters. Allen was determined that a more responsible attitude should be adopted by all who handled the mail:

> The by and way letters are thrown promiscuously together in one large bag, which was to be opened at every stage by the deputy or any other inferior servant of the house, to pick out of the whole heap whatever might belong to his own delivery, and the rest put back again into this large bag, with such by letters as he should have to send to distant places from his own stage.

Allen organised the cross-posts from his home at Bath, but when he died in 1764 the organisation was transferred to the care of the Post Office in London.

Under the Act of 1765 towns could set up local Penny Posts, and gradually many places began to establish this facility. Dublin began a Penny Post in 1773, followed by such places as Edinburgh, Leith, Manchester, Bristol, Liverpool and Birmingham. By 1840 more than 350 towns in England and Wales had their own Penny Posts, and these posts performed a vital public service to those living within the areas covered. The Penny Posts served the villages nearby; almost 1,500 villages in England and Wales were provided with postal services.

Letters sent by the General Post were often collected by the people they were addressed to at the post office in the town; but, if delivered by letter-carriers, an extra charge (the delivery penny) was often exacted. In 1774 it was ruled that the Post Office must deliver letters without charging an additional fee (as was already the case in London, Edinburgh and Dublin) inside the boundaries of a post town. This was the beginning of a free delivery service recognised by law. It was much later before the villages and remote parts of the country received the same privilege. The Postmaster General fixed the boundary within which the free delivery of letters would operate. In 1843 it was agreed that there should be a free daily delivery to any place that received at least 100 letters a week. In 1850 it was decided that posts must pay their way, and this resulted in the posts for some areas being sent only twice or three times a week, and in some cases even weekly. But these were remote cases. By 1862, 94 per cent of all postal matter was delivered at the ordinary postage charge. Finally, in 1897, free regular deliveries were provided everywhere.

FURTHER READING
F. Staff, *The Penny Post, 1680–1918*

3 The Mail-Coach Era

During the seventeenth century letters were carried, illegally, by owners of wagons. Hackney-coaches too were known to carry 'multitudes of letters'. Speeds achieved, however, were slow, mainly because of the state of the roads. Turnpikes were set up in a few places in the seventeenth century, but it was not until the eighteenth century that they became really widespread, and then the roads were often little improved. As late as the first decade of the nineteenth century, Daniel Paterson, a travel writer, gave this warning about the roads:

> It is recommended to all travellers to make previous inquiry into the state of them, as many of the cross turnpike roads are, in winter, and often after wet weather, rendered almost impassable.

Thus, stagecoaches, which were privately run ventures, were often unreliable; the Birmingham to London service, advertised as making the journey in 2½ days, ran 'if God permit'. Improvements to the roads throughout the country were slow, but they were consistent if gradual, from the second half of the eighteenth century onwards. The improvement in road construction was largely the result of the work of experts such as Telford, Macadam and Metcalfe.

It was John Palmer who realised that mail-coaches could be used to carry letters. Palmer was born at Bath, and through Bath ran one of the best roads in the country, the route between London and Bristol. A stage-coach at the time when Palmer outlined his plan was able to complete the 120 miles in about 17

Ashton-under-Line P·P

SHAFTESBURY Penny Post

BRISTOL PENNY POST

Warwick Penny Post

8 Some penny post handstamps.

PEEBLES PENNY POST

Derry Penny Post

hours. Palmer's idea was to have mail-coaches running all over the country: 'Where new roads are now continually making, and villages growing into great manufacturing towns, the Post of such a country must be open to continual variation and improvement.'

Palmer based his plan on the fact that stage-coaches were able to travel so much faster and safer than postboys. A postboy on horseback who left Bath for London late on Monday night did not reach the capital until Wednesday afternoon. But a coach that left Bath on Monday afternoon (and which illegally carried letters) arrived in London at about ten o'clock on Tuesday morning. Palmer had little praise for the postboys, and thought it ridiculous that letters were sent by 'some idle boy without character, mounted on a worn-out hack, who so far from being able to defend himself or escape from a robber, is more likely to be in league with him'.

Mail sent by postboys paid no road tolls, and Palmer suggested that the same should apply to mail-coaches which would help to increase their speed as they would have no need to stop. The keeper would open the tollgate when he heard the horn of the mail-coach sound in the distance. Palmer presented his plan to William Pitt in 1782, but it was not until 1784 that his proposals were accepted. There were some in the Post Office who were very much against the plan of sending letters by mail-coach. One Post Office surveyor believed that the necessary stops along the way could not be shortened, as postmasters had to open bags of mail to take out bundles and add others. The same official was also uncertain that mail-coaches would stop robbery on the highway, for it was believed that desperate thieves would still attempt hold-ups:

9 The General Post Office Sorting Office at Lombard Street in 1809.

10 John Palmer of Bath as a youth. He thought of sending letters by coach instead of postboys. This speeded up the flow of mail and made it more secure in transit. Later, lighter mail coaches were constructed specially for this purpose.

It was lately the case upon the North Road, where an iron cart, as strong as an iron chest, was stopt, taken out of the road and broke open. . . . When desperate fellows had once determined upon a mail robbery, the consequence would be murder in case of resistance.

But experience showed that the fears of this surveyor were groundless: attacks on mail-coaches were extremely rare.

Palmer's measures included an increase in postage which he believed to be justified by the speedier delivery offered. A letter from London to Edinburgh now cost 7d. instead of 6d. Mail-coaches were exempted from toll charges in 1785. Palmer was present when the first mail-coach left Bristol on 2 August 1784. Extensions followed quickly: in 1785 there were mail-coach services to Liverpool, Manchester, Leeds, Swansea, Dover, Oxford, Chester and Carlisle, to name but a few. The service was extended to Edinburgh in the following year, when the journey of just over 400 miles was completed in 60 hours. At first, ordinary stage-coaches were used as mail-coaches, but only a limited number of passengers were carried, in order not to slow the service down. Four were allowed inside the coach and usually about three on the top, with the driver and the guard. One traveller wrote to his wife of his journey on the mail-coach from London to Edinburgh which travelled at over seven miles an hour: 'You can only get a very piecemeal view of the country from the windows, and on account of the tremendous speed, you have no object long in view.' The Chief Justice, Lord Campbell, journeyed along the Great North Road from the Edinburgh end, and later wrote of the perils of fast travelling:

. . . this speed was thought to be highly dangerous to the head, independently of the perils of an overturn, and stories were told of men and women who, having reached London with such celerity, died suddenly of an infection of the brain. My family and friends were seriously alarmed for me, and advised me at all events to stay a day in York to recruit myself. . . . I boldly took my place all the way through to London.

Palmer had succeeded in getting established a fast, improved mail service. He was rewarded by the office of Surveyor and Comptroller General of the Mails in 1786, at a salary of £1,500 a year, plus a bonus for increases in Post Office revenue above a certain sum.

The government had to finance from somewhere the heavy expenses incurred in the Napoleonic Wars, and the Post Office revenue was the target of attack on more than one occasion. Further changes occurred in the rates of postage in 1801, 1805 and also in 1812, when the lowest charge for a single letter sent through the General Post, for a distance not exceeding 15 miles, was 4d. At the other end of the scale, letters that travelled for more than 700 miles paid 17d. Mileage marks were introduced on postmarks, indicating the distance that a particular post office was from London – York, for instance, had a mileage mark of 196, Nottingham of 127, and Glasgow of 405. It was thus possible to calculate the cost of a letter swiftly, and to dispatch it without delay. Mileage marks survived until a uniform rate of postage for the whole country was introduced in 1840.

By 1812 there were more than 200 mail-coaches in use. All of them were exempt from tolls, as too were the passengers. Stage-coach owners and owners of turnpikes wanted mail-coaches to pay the same toll as other vehicles, complaining with some justification that the mail-coaches took some of the best passenger traffic, yet paid nothing for the wear and tear on the roads which they helped to cause. In England the mail-coach retained its privileged position, but in Scotland the Act of 1813 enforced tolls from all vehicles with more than two wheels. This toll was responsible for an increase in postal charges of a halfpenny for letters carried by mail-coaches in Scotland.

Under the Post Office Act of 1711, Post Office surveyors had been appointed whose original duty was to check distances on the post roads. Letters were charged partly by distance, so it was thought that distances between towns should be recorded as accurately as possible. Later, it was realised that some sort of on-the-road check was needed on the accounts of postmasters, the activities of postboys, and alleged robberies, so in 1715 six surveyors were appointed, one of them for each of the six main post roads. The office of Post Office surveyor lasted until 1940.

11 The Worcester Mail in 1805.

Here is an extract from the journal of the surveyor for the South-Western District for 1789:

Jan. 29th, 30th and 31st. – At Exeter to give directions about the irregularity of the different mails there on account of the Snow and Frost, and seeing them in and out, and giving all the Guards proper directions about their duty in case of the like, also with the Postmaster of Crediton – 3 days.

Feb. 2nd to 28th. – On the Road at the various Offices and Stages betwixt Exeter, Salisbury and London during the Snow and extreme bad state of the road, to keep the Coaches to regularity and to see the different Branch mails in, from thence to London attending the Comptroller General and giving him an account of the regulations made, as well as to consult him on future improvements, and back to Reading, Bath and Warminster – 27 days.

There were close on 20 mail-coach routes in Scotland, some of which were the fastest in Britain. Speeds had to be competitive because of the ever-present stage-coaches that were only too eager to take passengers from the mail-coaches if they could manage it. Mail-coaches in England and Scotland were organised by the Superintendent of the Mail-coaches, centred in London. All the mail-coaches in Britain were supplied by one contractor in an attempt to establish a uniform and well-constructed pattern. Finch Vidler, for instance, held the monopoly to supply mail-coaches for more than four decades until 1836, when the supply of

12 A mail-coach leaving the G.P.O. early in the nineteenth century. Mail coaches travelled at night and left London for the provinces in the evening.

13   The 'Quicksilver' Royal Mail-coach on the Devonport to London route.

mail-coaches was opened to competition. The first mail-coaches had been stage-coaches, but the later ones were specially constructed to travel light and fast. Contractors for the mail routes hired the coaches from Vidler for 2½d. a double mile. Vidler's staff was on hand to take charge when the coaches returned at the end of a run. They were cleaned carefully, greased, and delivered in travelling condition at the coaching inns ready for the next run.

Mail-coaches travelled at night. At one time, the mail had left London after midnight and it was Palmer who suggested that the mail coaches should leave at eight o'clock in the evening instead. This practice was adopted.

There were some large-scale coaching contractors at work in London who, in addition to supplying mail-coaches, also owned many stage-coaches. One such contractor, Chaplin, had 150 horses stabled at the Crown and Cushion Inn for his stage-coach and mail services. At one point, he owned about 70 coaches and 1,800 horses. About half the 28 different mail-coaches that left London each night were drawn by horses supplied by Chaplin. Such large numbers of horses were

14   The Bath Mail-coach receiving the postbag from a post office along the route.

needed because of the frequent changes that were necessary when the horses travelled at speed. An average run was only about 10 miles, so on a 400-mile run from London to Edinburgh there would be at least 40 changing points. Often there was the equivalent of a horse a mile along important routes, and, even at this seemingly generous rate, it was found necessary to replace about a third of the horses each year.

The change of horses (two minutes were allowed) and of driver – for he too was replaced each 30–40 miles – had to be accomplished with all speed, and even the mail guard had to help if things looked safe. Of course, the main job of this Post Office employee was to guard the letters carried on the coach. The mail was locked in a fixed box positioned at his feet and he sat outside the coach at the back. He carried a blunderbuss, pistols and a cutlass. If there was trouble, or if the coach broke down, the guard might take one of the horses and the mail and ride on with it. In addition, the guard had a horn to blow to announce the arrival of the coach, and also a locked timepiece which had to be handed over when he reached the end of his part of the run. This helped to keep coaches running to schedule, but as there was not as yet standard time, London's time being 20 minutes ahead of Bristol's, the time shown on the timepiece had to be adjusted on the east–west routes depending on the direction of travel. Even when coach construction improved, the ride was still far from smooth, and on occasions guards were thrown off on a particularly rough stretch of road, and perhaps not missed for some time! Mail-coach guards wore scarlet uniforms, braided with gold, and three-cornered hats. The drivers were similarly dressed. The guard earned 13 shillings gross a week, but three shillings were deducted for uniform, pension and sick pay.

Stage-coaches were painted brightly and had eye-catching names such as 'Defiance', 'Telegraph', 'Greyhound' and 'Comet'. The mail-coaches were painted black and maroon, and had the name of the route; and the four Royal orders were on the upper panels and on the doors.

The Bristol run left London at 8 p.m. and arrived at Bath at 6.32 a.m. the next morning, and at Bristol at 7.45 a.m. On one occasion, Gladstone needed to get from Torquay to Newark in a hurry on a Sunday, and his route from Exeter, using mail-coach and stage, is worth careful note:

Mail to London. Conversation with a tory countryman who got in for a few miles, on Sunday travelling, which we agreed in disapproving. . . . Excellent mail. Dined at Yeovil . . . at $6\frac{1}{2}$ a.m. arrived at Piccadilly, $18\frac{1}{2}$ hours from

15 The scene outside St Martin's le Grand in the nineteenth century. This office was the hub of the postal system of the country.

16 An early railway sorting carriage, 1838.

Exeter. Went to Fetter Lane, washed and breakfasted, and came off at 8 o'clock by a High Flyer for Newark. . . . Tea at Stamford; arriving at Newark at midnight.

On Gladstone's journey the mail travelled faster than the stage. Mail-coach drivers were complimented frequently on their care, but there were exceptions. In the 1830s the Holyhead mail tried to pass the Chester mail near St Albans. The Chester mail driver was furious, and pulled his leading horses – mail coaches usually had four horses – across the other's path, causing a collision in which one of the passengers was killed. Both drivers were imprisoned for a year.

The longest run in Britain was from London to Thurso, covering a distance of 783 miles. Letters and passengers too (if they had the strength!) could leave London, say, on Monday; reach Edinburgh on Wednesday afternoon; and Thurso on Friday at 6 p.m. It is difficult now to understand how eagerly news was looked for. For instance, the Battle of Trafalgar was fought on 21 October 1805. The 'Pickle' served as the messenger ship that carried news of the victory back to England. It set sail on 27 October, and by 4 November it was off Falmouth nearing the end of its 1,000-mile journey from the south of Spain. The captain set off for London on horseback carrying Collingwood's messages. With hard riding, the journey took two nights. The news reached the Admiralty early in the morning on 6 November. *The Times* for 7 November (in which news of the victory is told to the nation) records: 'Yesterday morning at eight o'clock, a messenger was sent off with despatches to his Majesty at Windsor, with the joyful news of the late victory.'

Frederic Hill, brother of Rowland, tells how Birmingham received news of the Battle of Waterloo:

> Every one was aware that a great battle must be taking place, and while the result was yet unknown, we were all on the tiptoe of eager expectation. On the morning of the day when the decisive news was expected, many people stationed themselves far out on the London road to get the first view of the approaching mail-coach. When at last it dashed into Birmingham, covered with waving boughs of laurel, there was a great shout.

In a mere 60 years the idea of carrying letters by mail-coach had been conceived, developed and as quickly ended. Just as the postboy had been superseded by the mail-coach, so the mail-coach was replaced by the railway. Letters were first carried by train in 1830 on the Manchester to Liverpool route. By 1837 there were four mails a day between these centres. Mail-coaches travelled at 10 miles an hour, railways at 20 miles an hour at that time, so the time they took in transporting mail, as well as people and goods, was halved. In September 1838, the Birmingham–London line was opened. The last daily run of the London coach to Norwich and Newmarket took place in 1846. The last mail-coach left Manchester in 1858. Mail-coaches survived longer in more distant places, such as the west of England, Ireland and Scotland. The splendour of the mail-coach era passed quickly, but was remembered nostalgically by coachmen and others long after the coaches ceased to operate.

FURTHER READING
J. T. Foxell and A. O. Spafford, *Monarchs of All they Surveyed: The Story of the Post Office Surveyors*

4 Sending Letters before 1840

The Post Office could be cheated in four main ways: official dishonesty; the abuse of the franking system; cheating about payment; and illegal carriers.

There were dishonest agreements between different postmasters not to declare all the letters carried, and to enter incorrect returns in their accounts. In an effort to prevent similar agreements between postmasters and sorters, the sorters in London were not allowed to open bags from the same place for consecutive arrivals. Both postboys and coachmen carried letters secretly in their pockets, charging their own rates of postage for doing so. Official letters were carried inside heavy bags, which in turn held small canvas bags that contained the letters from each post town on the road.

Most postboys were not boys, in fact, though some were youths – 'Many of whom are barely 14 years of age'. More commonly, they were grown men capable of handling horses well, often old cavalry soldiers. Postboys sometimes were in collusion with highwaymen, though this might be difficult to prove. If proof became available, both were hanged. Towards the end of the eighteenth century the Warrington and Chester postboy was robbed, and though the two highwaymen who robbed him were later hanged many postboys became reluctant to ride along certain routes. The Postmaster of Chester had to send disturbing news to the District Surveyor as late as 1796:

> I beg leave to inform you the Post Boy that took the Mail from hence this morning for Preston and Liverpool, deserted it about two miles off, and tyed his horse to a tree. The Mail was found fastened to a Mail Pillion on the back of the horse, by two men going to work about half past 5 o'clock, and brought it back here all safe. I immediately sent the Mail forward, and informed the Deputys of Preston and Liverpool the cause of the delay. I will endeavour to find the young rascal and have him punished for his villainy.

The postboy in question was apprehended and given three weeks' hard labour as a punishment. The ease with which postboys were attacked was a source of constant worry to Francis Freeling, the Secretary of the General Post Office, and his recommendations for the proper protection of postboys were ultimately adopted:

> Each rider should be furnished with cutlass, brace of pistols, strong cap for the defence of his head, and once a year with a jacket of blue cloth with a red collar for the day, and a thick coat once in two years for the night.

Postal officials in receiving houses had to hold a letter up to the light or in front of a candle to find out how many sheets it contained in order to work out the postal charge. This procedure told them if the letter contained any valuables and put them in the way of temptation, a temptation not always resisted.

Sometimes letters were intercepted by the Post Office to get hold of information which the government wanted. Such letters were read and then sent on to their destinations, and there is some evidence that this practice may have been increasing in the first part of the nineteenth century. Warrants were issued and these gave the necessary authority to open letters. A letter sent to Jonathan Swift in the first part of the eighteenth century stated: 'If I do not write intelligibly to you, it is because I would not have the clerks of the post office know everything that I am doing.'

Another letter in the Swift correspondence contains this strange postscript:

To the gentlemen of the Post Office, who intercepted my last letter addressed to Mrs Whiteway at her house in Abbey Street. . . . When you have sufficiently perused this letter, I beg the favour of you to send it to the lady to whom it is directed. . . . I shall think myself obliged to you if, at the same time, you will

17 Pre-stamp covers. The upper cover contained an account only written on the other side of the paper, of course, yet the cost of sending it from London to Edinburgh was very high. The distance charge was 1s. 1d. plus an extra ½d. because the letter travelled in a mail coach in Scotland (top right-hand corner: Add ½); it is dated January 1816. The lower cover shows the back of a sheet that has been sealed with wax. This was the most common way to secure letters though many people used wafer seals bought for the purpose. This cover has been folded several times so that a long letter could be written on a single sheet, a necessary consideration when each sheet paid a separate charge.

be pleased to send Mrs Whiteway those letters which are now in your hands, with such alterations and amendments as you think proper, but I cannot believe that your order will justify you in detaining letters of business as . . . I conceive you have not a licence to rob on the highway.

This official snooping into private letters was criticised as late as 1844, when both Houses of Parliament appointed Secret Committees on the Post Office.

Important people such as Members of Parliament were allowed to send their letters free of charge. The sender merely had to sign his name at the bottom left-hand corner on the outside of the letter. This letter was stamped 'Free' by the Post Office and the holder of the privilege was said to have a free frank, the frank being the signing of the letter. Every year the Under-Secretary of State for the Colonies, Sir James Stephen, spent the equivalent in time of a whole month, working six hours a day, simply writing his signature on the outside of letters so that the Post Office would recognise them as free franks and allow them free passage through the post. Unfortunately, the concession was subject to many abuses. People with a free frank often signed many pieces of paper and gave them away to their friends who could send letters of their own free of charge by using the frank-holder's signature. Sometimes M.P.s and others who held franks even sold them or gave them away to constituents to curry favour. In consequence, the Post Office lost a great deal of money. It was estimated that five million franks were used annually by both Houses of Parliament. Horace Walpole, the eighteenth-century politician, was asked frequently to frank other people's letters: 'May I presume to beg the favour of you to frank the enclosed two letters which may go to the post office whenever your servant carries your own.'

Sir Walter Scott tells in a note in *Redgauntlet* that it was common to save franked covers and return them to be used again 'as long as the envelope could hold together'. When cheap postage for all was introduced in 1840 the system of free franks ceased, and even the frank of Queen Victoria ceased to be valid. From that time, the official letters sent by government officials still were allowed to pass through the post free of charge but in specially recognisable envelopes. You are sure to have seen the brown envelopes sent to your home about your parents' income tax returns with the words 'On Her Majesty's Service' printed across the top. Where the stamp would be, these envelopes have the words OFFICIAL PAID. Of course, it is still possible for a person to use these envelopes to post his own private letters, but if he does this today he knows that he is taking a serious risk, for if discovered he can be fined heavily. Franks are awarded occasionally today to particular people. When President John F. Kennedy was assassinated in 1963 his widow was given a free frank by the United States Government. This was done as a gesture of respect and also it allowed her to reply to the many thousands of letters of sympathy she received from all over the world.

Newsletters, the newspapers of today, had been distributed by post as a special privilege since the mid-seventeenth century. The names of many newspapers have

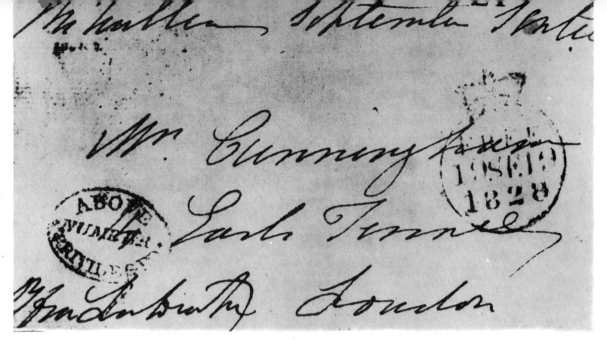

18 A free frank signed on the bottom left corner by the person who possessed the right to send letters free of postage. The cover is stamped FREE with the date in a circle surmounted by a crown. The stamp on the left shows that the letter was 'above number privileged'. It would appear from the number at the top on the right that it was the 21st letter posted by the owner of the frank that day.

postal connections – the Mail, the Telegraph and the Post. One such newsletter was the *London Gazette*, sent out from London by Post Office officials called Clerks of the Road, and under their franks. This privilege was extended, and the Clerks became entitled to frank any newspaper, whoever it was addressed to. In the eighteenth century the Clerks accepted subscriptions and undertook to supply newspapers throughout the country. Thus, they became newsagents. If newspapers had been sent letter rate, the postage would have been very heavy, so newspapers were sent by post under frank or not at all. In 1764, this privilege was acknowledged officially by statute, but M.P.s also were allowed to send newspapers free through the post. As in the case of free franks on sheets used as letters, the M.P.s soon found that this was a very profitable and easy way of making money. For a price, they granted free postage to booksellers and newsagents for their newspapers, and the charge became less than that of the Clerks of the Road. To try to stop the wholesale cheating that went on with franks, an Act of 1802 required M.P.s to sign on the packet the whole address and date of posting, and name the post town the newspaper was posted in. Also the M.P. had to be in the post town where newspapers were posted on the date of posting. The reasons for these measures are clear to see. The idea was to make it difficult for M.P.s to sign many packets personally (supposed to be the only legal way of doing so) and so make them cut down on the selling of the frank to those prepared to buy it. But the provisions of the Act were too difficult to maintain, and within a few years an

39

M.P.S name on a newspaper or wrapper – whether written by an M.P., someone else or even printed – was enough to secure free transmission of newspapers through the post. So nobody paid postage on newspapers. In 1825 newspapers became legally entitled to travel by post free of charge provided the tax had been paid. This was reduced in 1835, and abolished in 1870 when a postal charge of a halfpenny per newspaper was introduced.

The problem was that messages could be transmitted by sending a newspaper through the post. Some people pricked a few words in the newspaper with a pin, or wrote in invisible ink. It was impossible to examine each newspaper that went through the post, so most of these messages went undetected. Another way was to use a pre-arranged code. Rowland Hill, an important figure in nineteenth-century postal reform, tells of one of these codes:

Some years ago, when it was the practice to write the name of a member of parliament, for the purpose of franking a newspaper, a friend of mine, previous to starting a tour into Scotland, arranged with his family a plan for informing them of his progress and state of health, without putting them to the expense of postage. It was managed thus: He carried with him a number of old newspapers, one of which he put into the Post Office daily. The post-mark, with the date, showed his progress; and the state of his health was evinced by the

19 A bellman, 1820, who toured the streets with a bell to indicate his approach. He had a locked bag with a slit to receive letters from people who used him as a kind of walking pillar box, in the days before pillar boxes had been introduced. The last bellmen in London disappeared in 1846.

selection of the name, from a list previously agreed upon, with which the newspaper was franked – 'Sir Frank Burdett', I recollect, denoted vigorous health.

Later, Rowland Hill admitted that the 'friend' in this story was himself, and he explained further:

It must not be supposed that in franking these newspapers I was usurping a privilege. In those days newspapers, unless franked, at least in appearance, were charged as letters. But anyone was at liberty to use the name of any Peer or Member of Commons without his consent. The publishers of newspapers had a name printed on the wrapper.

Methods of sending trading details could be worked out easily in advance. If a trader in London wanted to let a colleague in Edinburgh know about changes in the market, say, in tea, he sent a newspaper and the way the name on the address was written stood for a day of the week, so Mr Smith meant Monday, Mr John Smith meant Tuesday, Mr J. Smith meant Wednesday and so on. Under the name there was a possible variety of business terms to be used – Tea Dealer, Grocer, etc. – each of which would indicate a particular occurrence. So a newspaper addressed to Mr Smith, Tea Dealer, would mean that on Monday the price of tea was rising.

The letters that most people sent through the post were supposed to be paid for, but payment, even then, was not always made. The postage on letters could be paid when they were handed in at the post office or it could be collected when the letter-carrier delivered the letters at their destinations. The second of these methods was by far the more usual. Letters were offered at houses in the first place, but if the occupants could not pay the letter-carrier, they were returned to the local post office until the money was produced. Today we should think it very rude if people posted letters to us without first paying the postage for them. Before 1840 most people saw things the other way round, perhaps thinking that more care would be taken of the letter if the Post Office did not get paid for carrying it until it was delivered. One postmaster reported:

The price of a letter is a great tax on poor people. I sent one, charged eightpence, to a poor labouring man about a week ago; it came from his daughter. He first refused taking it, saying it would take a loaf of bread from his other children; but, after hesitating a little time, he paid the money and opened the letter. I seldom return letters of this kind to Bristol, because I let the poor people have them, and take the chance of being paid; sometimes I lose the postage, but generally the poor people pay me by degrees.

This was a kindly postmaster, but not all of them could afford to take the risk of being so kind-hearted. Richard Cobden, of anti-corn law league fame, estimated

41

20 A letter carrier collecting postage at the door in the 1830s. The vast majority of letters were not pre-paid and the postage had to be collected when they were delivered. This wasted much time for the letter carrier in waiting for the money and in giving change. It was considered in many quarters to be rather impolite to pre-pay the letters one sent (unless perhaps to social inferiors) in the same way that it would be considered wrong to enclose a stamp for a reply today. Pre-payment did not become common until 1840.

that 'we have 50,000 Irish in Manchester who are almost as precluded as though they lived in New South Wales, from all correspondence with their relatives in Ireland'. The public, in fact, thought of many dodges to avoid paying for messages, other than those described already. Someone could go to the local post office where he knew there was a letter for him as soon as he could pay its postage. He could pretend to be about to pay the postage, and the clerk would get the letter and put it on the counter. This was where the recipient had to be quick. He could see at a glance who the letter was from by the handwriting of the address, and that in itself may be all he wanted to know. Then he could refuse to accept the letter. The following tale illustrates what could happen. The poet Samuel T. Coleridge relates:

> One day, when I had not a shilling which I could spare, I was passing a cottage not far from Keswick, where a letter-carrier was demanding a shilling for a letter, which the woman of the house appeared unwilling to pay, and at last declined to take. I paid the postage; and when the man was out of sight, she told me that the letter was from her son, who took that means of letting her know that he was well: the letter was *not to be paid for*. It was then opened and found to be blank!

There were many other ways of sending messages, for instance, by using coded signs on the outside of a letter. Usually, the letter-carrier was willing to allow a recipient to examine the outside of a letter before paying for it. The way in which the name or the address was written, which might appear to be harmless enough, perhaps with a line or a squiggle after it, or a particular colour ink, were merely some of the means employed of using coded messages without actually paying for the receipt of them. Some people went to the trouble of arranging detailed codes. There were literally hundreds of ways of writing a name and an address that looked honest enough but, in fact, held a hidden meaning. For instance, there are

42

more than 40 ways of spelling a variation on the surname Patterson, and over 100 ways of spelling a word which sounds like Ashley.

The Post Office also lost much revenue because of the activities of illegal carriers of letters. It was then, and still is today, a punishable offence for anyone but the Post Office to carry letters and to charge for doing so. But this did not stop the carriers. Many local carriers with a cart risked punishment and carried letters for those who paid for the service, but they charged much less than the Post Office did. Even drivers and guards of mail-coaches were not above joining in the illegal traffic of carrying letters other than through official channels. It became the sole business of some carriers to collect and distribute letters, which many of them did openly, without fearing prosecution. Sometimes women and children were employed to collect the letters. Much of the postal business of Glasgow, for example, passed through unofficial channels, and of Cirencester it was reported that:

> The people in that town did not think of using the post for the conveyance of letters . . . two carriers . . . carried four times as many letters as the mail did.

Instances of this kind could be multiplied. The Birmingham carriers of letters carried them up to 12 miles away at a penny a letter. Rowland Hill pointed out:

> I have been informed by a highly respectable merchant and manufacturer of Birmingham, that the number of letters distributed by these means very greatly exceeds, in his opinion, the number distributed within the same district by the Post Office.

Only occasionally were carriers prosecuted and fined. One carrier was caught and his bag contained 1,100 letters. Sometimes parcels were discovered full of letters. The parcel was sent to its destination, then opened and the unofficial carriers sorted and delivered the letters. Of course, the public supported the carriers and used their cheap services readily. It is of interest that the Post Office did not seem able to levy the full penalties against those carriers who were discovered. In 1833, though one of the fines was £1,000, the highest amount actually paid was only £160. Occasional prosecutions of individual carriers did not stop the system but merely showed how common it was in most parts of the country.

The opportunities for postal evasion appeared to increase as means of transport improved. This happened between England and Ireland with the rise of steam navigation. Railways carried many parcels which contained letters; a dozen trains daily ran between Manchester and Liverpool, and it was estimated that 500 letters could be parcelled and sent by train for a shilling! The same illegal system operated for foreign mails:

> The evasion of the postage on letters sent from different parts of the United

Kingdom to the out-ports, for the purpose of being put on board of ships bound for foreign parts, especially to the United States of America, is yet more remarkable than the evasion of the inland postage. It is thoroughly known to the Post Office authorities; but the practice appears to be winked at.

How great was the evasion of Post Office channels can be seen from the fact that when the regular steamship service opened between Liverpool and New York, only five letters were sent in the official Post Office bag; yet 10,000 letters were carried illegally by the same ship!

Whenever possible, people asked their friends who were going on journeys to carry a letter for them and to deliver it. Sometimes several messages were sent on the same sheet of paper:

> A shopkeeper in the country has occasion to transmit orders to two or more London tradesmen; these are frequently written on one large sheet, and addressed as a single letter to one party, who divides the sheet, and distributes the several parts.

Why, then, did people bother? Why go to such lengths to cheat the Post Office and save a few pence? Clearly, the answer lies in the very high rates of postage in Britain before 1840. The annual number of postal items carried in the 1830s was

chargeable letters	88,600,000
franked letters	7,400,000
newspapers	30,000,000
total	126,000,000

Today there are 40 million letters sent through the post *daily,* so more letters are now sent in four days than the total number of postal items sent in a *year* before 1840! Practically one out of every three items carried before 1840 did not pay to go through the post. Those letters that were chargeable often had to bear heavy rates. A letter was charged according to the number of sheets, and also depending on how far it was going. Letters were not often sent in envelopes, as an envelope counted as a sheet of paper and cost extra. Letters were written on large sheets which were folded over several times and then sealed at the back with wax or with a wafer. The address was written on the front of the cover. The longer the distance travelled by a letter, the more expensive was its postage. The minimum charge for sending a letter through the General Post (not the local Penny Posts) was 4d. But this did not take a letter very far. A letter sent from London to Brighton cost 8d., and one from London to Edinburgh cost 1s. 1½d. Each page in a letter paid as much as any other page. A three-page letter from London to Brighton paid two shillings. People tried to get their letters on large sheets and wrote small to save writing on another sheet.

Postal Charges.

Not exceeding 15 miles 4 pence
Above 15 but not exceeding 20 miles 5 ,,
,, 20 ,, ,, ,, 30 ,, 6 ,,
,, 30 ,, ,, ,, 50 ,, 7 ,,
,, 50 ,, ,, ,, 80 ,, 8 ,,
,, 80 ,, ,, ,, 120 ,, 9 ,,
,, 120 ,, ,, ,, 170 ,, 10 ,,
,, 170 ,, ,, ,, 230 ,, 11 ,,
,, 230 ,, ,, ,, 300 ,, 12 ,,
,, 300 ,, ,, ,, 400 ,, 13 ,,
,, 400 ,, ,, ,, 500 ,, 14 ,,
,, 500 ,, ,, ,, 600 ,, 15 ,,
,, 600 ,, ,, ,, 700 ,, 16 ,,
Above 700 miles 17 ,,

All these charges were for single letters: a single sheet of paper. Letters that consisted of two or three sheets had to pay double or treble charges. Think what a three or four-page letter from London to Edinburgh would cost! Letters sent from England into Scotland by a coach with more than two wheels had to pay an extra halfpenny. Additional rates were charged for carrying letters by packet boat between Holyhead and Dublin, 2d. Letters which crossed the Menai Bridge or the Conway Bridge each paid an extra penny. These charges put the postal service beyond the means of most people and it was not until the efforts of Rowland Hill and his fellow reformers that a cheap post was introduced. Another reason for the low numbers of letters carried was that many people still could not read or write. The Education Act of 1870, the milestone in English education, meant that, ultimately, all children would get the chance to go to school, but in the mid-nineteenth century there were very many people unable to put pen to paper.

FURTHER READING
S. Graveson (Editor), *Penny Postage Centenary*

5 Rowland Hill's Plan

Robert Wallace was the first Member of Parliament to sit for the Scottish town of Greenock, and he was strongly in favour of postal changes. His maiden speech in Parliament was a daring attack not only on the way the Post Office was organised but also on the fact that the many abuses detailed in the last chapter were allowed to go on virtually unchecked. Much to the annoyance of the Post Office authorities, Wallace repeated his criticisms in speech after speech, but at last they began to take effect, and a committee known as the Post Office Commission of Inquiry was set up to examine the postal question in detail. The mass of information and figures which it produced, often too detailed and complicated for most people to understand, was used to great effect by one man in the fight for postal reform. His name was Rowland Hill.

Rowland Hill was born at Kidderminster in 1795 and was the son of a schoolmaster who ran a private school. Later, the family moved to London and opened a still larger school there. Rowland Hill had several brothers who were to prove of immense value and help to him in his efforts to reform the Post Office. He himself was keenly interested in Mathematics and statistics. He heard about the work that Robert Wallace was doing and became engrossed in the idea himself. Wallace, glad of support for his campaign, used his free frank to send Hill a great

21 Robert Wallace, M.P., and an advocate of postal reform before Rowland Hill took up the cause.

number of government reports and documents about the Post Office. Hill set to work to read and study this mass of information, which was so great that it needed a cab to deliver it. This would have been a full-time job for anyone; the fact that Hill was working simultaneously as Secretary to the South Australian Commission makes his achievement in studying and analysing the postal system remarkable. It is important to remember that he was not employed by the Post Office and had never even been behind the scenes in the Post Office in London to find out just what went on there. He tried to do this, of course, but the Post Office officials were jealous of their power and organisation and were not going to have a stranger appearing from nowhere to tell them what to do.

Hill realised the many unfortunate side-effects of high postal charges. They kept relatives in ignorance of each other, even though they lived only a few miles apart. The postmaster at Banwell reported:

My father kept the post office many years; he is lately dead; he used to trust poor people very often with letters; they generally could not pay the whole charge. He told me – indeed, I know – he did lose many pounds by letting poor people have their letters. We sometimes return them to London in consequence of the inability of the persons to whom they are addressed raising the postage. We frequently keep them for weeks; and, where we know the parties, let them have them, taking the chance of getting our money. One poor woman once offered my sister a silver spoon to keep until she could raise the money; my sister did not take the spoon, and the woman came with the amount in a day or two and took up the letter. It came from her husband, who was confined for debt in prison; she had six children, and was very badly off.

Often men out of work tramped from town to town looking for a job. If postal charges had been lower, people seeking employment could have written to see if jobs existed before setting off on long, tiring journeys. Mr Henson, a hosier from Nottingham, said:

When a man goes on the tramp – i.e. when he travels in search of employment – he must either take his family with him, perhaps one child in arms, or else the wife must be left behind; and the misery I have known them to be in from not knowing what has become of the husband, because they could not hear from him, has been extreme. Perhaps the man, receiving only sixpence, has never had the means, upon the whole line, of paying tenpence for a letter, to let his wife know where he was.

The poor were denied, therefore, the right to send letters, and even those in much better material circumstances were distressed frequently by high postal charges. Rowland Hill remembered the time when the letter-carrier called with a letter and his mother did not have the money to pay for it; and Mr Henson, the hosier, instructed his wife only to accept letters at the door when she knew who they were from.

The letter-carrier doing his rounds had a very different task to perform from the postman of today. Postmen today deliver letters through letter-boxes and then walk on to the next house. In the 1830s there were no letter-boxes in front doors and the letter-carrier had to knock to deliver the letter and collect the postage at each house. The time this wasted was staggering, as evidence given before the Commissioners of Revenue Inquiry in 1828 reveals. There existed in London an early delivery of letters whereby, at the cost of a small annual charge, a letter-carrier would deliver post on his way to the more remote parts of his ordinary round. This completed, the letter-carrier would return later in the morning to collect the postage on the privileged mail. Mr Benjamin Critchett, Inspector of the Inland Letter-Carriers, was examined by the Inquiry on this point:

If a postman were to deliver the whole of his letters as he went along, not taking the money for any of them, and returned through his walk, and then collected the money, would they not all be delivered much earlier than they are now? – Certainly.

And would it require more hands to do it than are now employed? – No.

The man going back to receive the postage of the early letters must pass by the doors where he had delivered letters and received the Postage? – Yes. I will describe the operation in two or three districts this morning. I will take Lombard-street, where the number of letters that were delivered this morning was 637.

Are you speaking of the general delivery? – I am speaking of the total number of letters sorted for that district.

And that were carried out by Letter Carriers? – That were carried out by Letter Carriers this morning; there were 637 letters, the amount of postage £25 14s. 3d. Of this number of letters, 570 were delivered early.

Could you state the time within which they were delivered? – All in half an hour.

What o'clock would that be? – That would be about half-past nine.

They were delivered in half an hour from the time they were dispatched? – From the time they were dispatched: 570 were delivered early, the postage £22 19s. 4d.; and 67 delivered in the ordinary way, postage £2 14s. 11d.

What time were they delivered? – Why, they would occupy the Letter Carrier about an hour and a half; then he commenced collecting the postage of the early delivery.

What! would he be an hour and a half in delivering 67 letters? – Yes, he would thereabouts.

Considering the extent of the district? – Yes, the time he would wait to get the money for a letter would be about two minutes to a house.

Have you made any calculation? – Yes, I have one at the office.

Two minutes at every house? – Yes; indeed some houses detain him at the door three, or four, or five minutes, in giving change, and various circumstances arise in the delivery of letters that detain the Letter Carriers.

Thus, half an hour was the time it took to deliver 570 letters when the postage was collected later. But 90 minutes were needed to deliver only 67 letters when the postage was collected at the same time. One form of delivery was about 25 times as fast as the other!

Rowland Hill set out his ideas in 1837 in a pamphlet of more than 100 pages which he called *Post Office Reform – Its Importance and Practicability*. Though he was responsible for the plan outlined in this important pamphlet, his brothers were of tremendous help to him during its composition, as they criticised his plan at each stage. Hill's principal aim was a simple one – he wanted pre-payment of letters when the Post Office accepted them, and he wanted a low, uniform rate of postage for letters posted from and to post towns. Whilst searching amongst so

22   Rowland Hill who fought for postal reform with the aid of hard facts gleaned from many sources. The publication of his pamphlet *Post Office Reform* in 1837 was the real beginning of the attack on the mandarins of St Martin's.

many Post Office reports Hill discovered facts from which he showed unquestionably that the distance a letter travelled did not cost more than a small fraction of a penny, whether that letter travelled round the corner or to the far end of the British Isles. The expensive part of the cost was in dealing with each letter separately when the Post Office accepted responsibility for it. Hill was convinced that if the cost of sending letters dropped, then far more of them would be sent. He used this simple economic argument to show that this would result, in the end, in a much larger postal revenue for the government than before. The important question to be worked out was: how could letters be pre-paid under such a scheme? The plan must prevent cheating on the part of postal clerks for there must be little opportunity for these people to keep any of the money they received. Charles Knight, a publisher, had suggested that newspapers could be placed inside stamped wrappers which would be sold at post offices for this purpose and Hill realised that this suggestion could be extended to letters. Hill thought of yet another way of pre-paying postage, that of having small pieces of sticky paper which could be stuck on the outside of a letter to denote that the postage had been paid. This was how he conceived such a scheme:

> A piece of paper just large enough to bear the stamp, and covered at the back with a glutinous wash, which the bringer might, by applying a little moisture, attach to the back of the letter.

In this single sentence, so casually expressed, Rowland Hill had invented the postage stamp. He realised that if this plan was followed, and postage paid at the start of a letter's journey, the letter-carrier would simply have to deliver the letters, which would speed up his round considerably. Hill made another revolutionary suggestion for improving efficiency:

> There would not only be no stopping to collect the postage, but probably it would soon be unnecessary even to await the opening of the door, as every house might be provided with a box into which the Letter-Carrier would drop the letters, and, having knocked, he would pass on as fast as he could walk.

Hill's proposals met with much opposition. The Postmaster General, Lord Lichfield, said:

> With respect to the plan set forth by Mr Hill, of all the wild and visionary schemes I have ever heard or read of, it is the most extravagant.

Colonel William Maberly, Secretary of the Post Office, was one of Hill's most important and powerful critics. Many Parliamentarians were against the plan, including the Duke of Wellington, as they were afraid that their precious franking privileges might end.

Hill's supporters, although numerous – they naturally included the public, and people such as businessmen and lawyers who sent many letters and had much to gain from cheap postage – by and large lacked the power and influence to further his scheme. However, Henry Cole, Secretary to the Mercantile Committee, an organisation of London merchants who were pressing for cheap postage, hit on a clever way of ridiculing the Post Office. The Committee wanted to send letters encouraging others in different parts of the country to support postal reform, but the high cost of sending letters made this very expensive. Cole overcame the problem by means of a newsletter called the 'Post Circular', which he had registered as a newspaper and as such subject to only a penny postage. The Post Office thus had to carry newsletters criticising itself, to people all over the country! Henry Cole wanted people to understand just how ridiculous were the rates of postage, and particularly the regulation which counted each sheet of paper as a separate letter. Cole tells in his Autobiography that on one occasion 100 letters were prepared, 50 of them on large single pieces of paper which were folded several times and sealed, the other 50 each consisting of two very thin sheets of paper which weighed very little:

Fifty of each specimen were sent to the Charing Cross Post Office, by a clerk who had some humour. He produced first one of the largest letters. The clerk looked at it suspiciously. He held it before the lamp to see if it were really a single sheet. He summoned another clerk to help his judgement. All this caused a delay, and a crowd began to collect at the window, and watched the process with interest. At last the clerk marked it with a *single* rate, and the spectators laughed. Then the smallest letter was produced, and the Post Office official turned crimson, became furious and cursed a little, but he could not help marking it *double* postage. Roars of laughter came from the crowd. Then fifty more of each letter were produced, and marked, the large heavy ones with *single* postage, the little light ones with *double*. During the process the crowd

23 Rowland Hill was assisted by the able Henry Cole who helped to ridicule the postal charges, both in stories and in sketches. This sketch of Cole's shows the Edinburgh mail coach loaded with newspapers and free franks, neither of which paid postage. The bag of letters on which postage was to be paid was conspicuous for its dimensions.

GREAT WEIGHT AND NO PRICE! LITTLE WEIGHT AND ALL PRICE!!

impatiently filled up the whole pavement and scoffed. No less amusement was produced in the House of Commons when Mr Wallace exhibited the big and little letters.

The most important postal reformers of the time were, therefore, a three-man team each with his own particular part to play. Robert Wallace dealt with the parliamentary side of things and pressed for legislative change. Rowland Hill presented the facts in such a way that it was difficult to dispute them. Henry Cole organised the Mercantile Committee and helped to influence public opinion in an important way. Each of these men played a vital part in the fight for postal changes which occurred eventually in 1840.

The government was firmly against such change as Hill outlined. It was true that he had been called before a Post Office enquiry, and later a Select Committee began to sit, in November 1837, but little came from these official investigations. At last, however, the Prime Minister had to agree to postal change. Agitation and petitions had grown greatly, and the press kept up a lively commentary on Hill's work. Low postal charges were carried by the Commons in the summer of 1839. Hill was asked to resign his position with the South Australian Commission to help the government to carry his plan smoothly, which he agreed to do.

A competition was announced in September 1839 to establish the best method of pre-paying postal charges. Many strange entries were received for this Treasury Competition, the vast majority of the 2,600 entries being ideas for stamped covers and wrappers. Only 49 of the entries were plans for adhesive postage stamps. Though four of the entries were judged joint winners (including one from Henry Cole) none of these suggestions were used ultimately. The final designs for the first stamps – the Penny Black and the Twopenny Blue – were not completed until 1840.

From 10 January 1840 penny postage was to be introduced on all letters up to half an ounce in weight. This was to be a pre-paid charge. Letters sent unpaid, paid double. Before then, for a few weeks, from 5 December 1839 to 9 January 1840, there was to be an intermediate period of a 4d. rate, except in the London district where the rate was to be one penny. This short period would allow post office officials to get used gradually to more customers, before the great rush of business that was expected when penny postage was extended to the whole country on 10 January. Nearly half the correspondence of the country passed through the London Post Office, and so the intermediate period would provide useful experience for the staff in coping with increased amounts of business and familiarising themselves with new procedures.

FURTHER READING
R. Hill, *Post Office Reform*
G. B. Hill, *Life of Rowland Hill*

6 1840 – the Year of Change

Rowland Hill began his official work to implement the postal changes on 16 September 1839. He was appointed to the Treasury, not to the Post Office. Although he was thereby shielded from his many opponents in the Post Office, he must have found it irritating to be unable to give direct orders and instructions to Post Office officials, and to have to endure the annoying delays while his plans were passed on by others. Hill wanted to have Henry Cole as his assistant at the Treasury, and it was agreed that Cole could leave his work as Assistant Keeper at the Record Office to be 'lent' to the Treasury for a while to assist Hill. Hill had journeyed to Paris in October 1839 to examine the postal system in operation there, which he found similar to that of London, except that the mail was handled by a smaller staff.

On 10 January uniform penny postage was extended throughout the country. The franking system ended on 9 January. The Post Office regulations stated that on and after 10 January a letter not exceeding half an ounce in weight could be sent from any part of the United Kingdom to any other part for one penny if paid when posted, or for two pence if paid when delivered. The public rushed to send cheap letters and, of course, to pre-pay the postage on them. Otherwise they would have cost double to send. Henry Cole visited the Head Post Office at St Martin's le Grand soon after penny postage had been introduced, and later wrote the following account of what he saw there:

A night or two after the change to a penny we ourselves witnessed the scene at St Martin's le Grand. The great hall was nearly filled with spectators, marshalled in a line by the police to watch the crowds pressing, scuffling, and fighting to get first to the window. The superintending President of the Inland Office with praiseworthy zeal was in all quarters directing the energy of his officers where the pressure was greatest. Formerly one window sufficed to receive letters. On this evening six windows with two receivers at each were bombarded by applicants. As the last quarter of an hour approached, and the crowd still thickened, a seventh window was opened, and that none might be turned away Mr Bokenham made some other opening, and took in money and letters himself. To the credit of the Post Office not a single person lost the time; and we learnt that on this evening upwards of 3,000 letters had been posted at St Martin's le Grand between five and six. A witness present on the first night of the Penny Post described to us a similar scene. When the window closed, the mob, delighted at the energy displayed by the officers, gave one cheer for the Post Office, and another for Rowland Hill.

24 A Treasury Competition entry from 1839. The entry is by Charles Fenton Whiting, one of the four prize-winners, and it shows the impracticability which was typical of many of the suggestions received. In this case, its size was against it. Note the VR 1d. POST PAID. It is interesting to note that the first stamps could well have been multi-coloured as this entry is white, red and black. Whiting was one of the most able entrants, submitting many ideas, and the intricacy of his design is well-illustrated in this photograph.

More than 300 towns made their own handstamps, which denoted that the postage had been paid on letters. In some places the old way of writing on the cover in ink the cost of sending the letter still continued, and it was not until 1853 that finally it became obligatory everywhere to use adhesive postage stamps. These were not available to the public until May 1840. It is remarkable that of the 2,600 entries received for the Treasury Competition not a single one was considered good enough to be brought into use, though doubtless these entries gave Rowland Hill and his colleagues useful ideas for future plans. It would appear that Rowland Hill had his own plan for the design of the stamps, for unofficial negotiations were taking place with the firm that eventually printed the first stamps as early as July 1839. When one remembers that the Treasury Competition was not announced until September 1839, and that this printing firm did not even enter for it, it would appear that Rowland Hill's decision, at least, was already made. Certainly, it would appear that Rowland Hill was not even consulted about the Treasury Competition in the first place. Many of the entries had been patterns which incorporated complicated designs that would be difficult to forge. But it was decided that something more than a pattern was needed. Benjamin Cheverton, one of the prize-winners, urged that the design for the stamps should be of a face:

> Now it so happens that the eye being educated to the perception of differences in the features of the face, the detection of any deviation in the forgery would be more easy – the difference of effect would strike an observer more readily than in the case of letters or any mere mechanical or ornamental device, although he may be unable, perhaps to point out where the difference lies, or in what it consists.

And who better to be the subject of the new stamps than the young Queen Victoria? The profile of Victoria chosen for these stamps was based on a portrait made when she was still a princess, and which later appeared on the medal designed by William Wyon, chief designer to the Royal Mint. This medal was made in 1837 to commemorate the Queen's official visit to the Guildhall after her Coronation. Sketches were made of the portrait on this medal by Henry Corbould, and from these the engravers Charles Heath and Frederick, his son, engraved the die for the first stamps. It took many months of hard work before the engraving was considered good enough. The first stamps were printed from line-engraved plates by the firm of Perkins, Bacon and Co. The engraver cut into the soft steel, in the reverse of the actual pattern, and the die was hardened. A soft steel roller was passed over it and impressions from it were transferred to the roller. This transfer roller was hardened and heavily but carefully rolled over a steel plate so that there were 240 impressions, all the same on one plate, in 20 rows of 12. This is the same number of stamps found on a sheet of definitives today.

The paper for the stamps was specially made by hand, in the presence of an officer of the Inland Revenue. Each sheet had to be accounted for so that none would fall into the hands of forgers. The sheets were counted into packs of 500 and sent to Somerset House. When they arrived they were counted again and then

TO ALL POSTMASTERS
AND
SUB-POSTMASTERS.

GENERAL POST OFFICE,
25th April, 1840.

IT has been decided that Postage Stamps are to be brought into use forthwith, and as it will be necessary that every such Stamp should be cancelled at the Post Office or Sub-Post Office where the Letter bearing the same may be posted, I herewith forward, for your use, an *Obliterating Stamp*, with which you will efface the Postage Stamp upon every Letter despatched from your Office. *Red Composition* must be used for this purpose, and I annex directions for making it, with an Impression of the Stamp.

As the Stamps will come into operation by the *6th of May*, I must desire you will not fail to provide yourself with the necessary supply of Red Composition by that time.

Directions for Preparing the Red Stamping Composition.

1 lb. Printer's Red Ink.
1 Pint Linseed Oil.
Half-pint of the Droppings of Sweet Oil.
To be well mixed.

By Command,

W. L. MABERLY,
SECRETARY.

25 Maberly's notice to postmasters. Note the recipe!

sent to the printers. The paper was greyish-white and was watermarked with 240 small crowns, one crown for each stamp. The watermarks were made by using hand-made wire crowns, so often there are slight differences in their shapes.

The stamps were printed on hand-operated presses, which turned out about 500 sheets a day. Again, an officer from the Inland Revenue was always present during the printing. He had to take the first sheets of stamps from a new printing plate to the Inland Revenue Department at Somerset House; there they were preserved as originals to refer to in cases of forgery. These first sheets still exist and, of course, are extremely valuable.

The printers applied the gum – or cement as it was called – to the back of sheets of stamps with brushes. The gum was dextrine, made by heating starch to a temperature of several hundred degrees. It did not taste very pleasant and was not a very good adhesive either. In fact, the government and not the printers were to blame. The printers supplied the stamps and gummed them by this cheap means (on the special paper sent to them by the government) at $7\frac{1}{2}$d. per thousand. If the government had wanted better gum they could have had it but the cost would have been higher. The Penny Blacks were put on sale in London on 1 May 1840 – the Twopenny Blues were available a few days later – though neither was supposed to be used until 6 May. In fact, a few stamps were sent through the post dated from 2 May onwards and because of their rarity they are especially valuable. The stamps were issued imperforate on sheets of 240. They had to be cut apart with scissors or torn from the sheet as they were required. Many clerks in the post

26   A Penny Black on cover cancelled in black with a Maltese Cross.

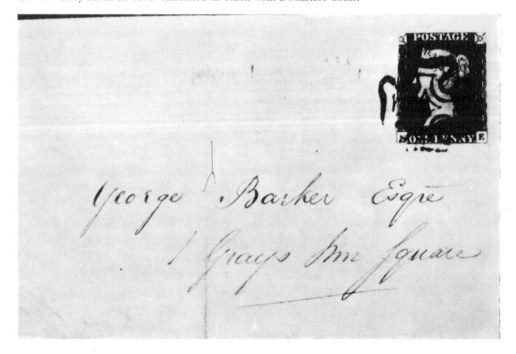

27 A Mulready envelope showing Mulready's design which was ridiculed in many quarters. It did not leave a great deal of space for the address.

offices at the start of each day cut the sheets of stamps into rows of 12 so that they would be easier to distribute to customers. Probably this is why stamp collectors find it easier to acquire parts of strips of these early stamps rather than blocks of them from several different rows. Letters were punched into the lower corners of each stamp on the plates, and no pair of letters on a plate were the same. These corner letters were punched in position individually and were a deterrent to a would-be forger, for then he would have to prepare a plate with different corner letters for each stamp or risk detection. The first row of letters began AA in the first stamp, then AB, AC and so on to the twelfth stamp in the first row which was lettered AL. The second row began BA, BB, BC etc., and this process was repeated to the last row which began TA and ended TL. The Penny Black had a life of under a year before it was replaced by a different stamp, but even in that short time more than 68 million of them were printed. The vast majority were destroyed by the public at once. Few people were interested in preserving them, as stamp-collecting as a hobby was as yet in the future. Perhaps some six millions of all those printed have survived to the present. Their value today varies, depending on their condition, and which of the 12 printing plates they came from. A very good Penny Black today costs several pounds, but one with edges rather imperfectly cut into the stamp can be bought for about a pound.

In a circular sent to all postmasters, Colonel Maberly, Secretary of the Post

28 A caricature of the Mulready design which poked fun at the original design by crudely copying its basic features.

Office, made this rather business-like statement in July 1840 showing that the department was tightening up on efficiency:

> It has been determined not to supply a fresh stock [of stamps] to such Post-masters who may be a month's revenue in arrear. In such cases the Postmaster General will be forced to resort to severe measures, as the parties must evidently be deeply in arrear to the department, while by their culpable neglect in not remitting they will inflict upon the whole of their neighbourhood the inconvenience of obtaining its stamps from other and more distant quarters.

Letters that were sent unstamped or incorrectly stamped had to pay at their destination twice the amount of the postage outstanding. This procedure still exists today – the double postage is a kind of fine for wasting the postman's time. It is difficult to understand what it must have been like before 1840 when almost all letters that had to pay postage were sent unpaid, and the letter-carrier had to stop and collect the money at each house. From 1840, at first the amount of postage to be collected on those letters that were not properly paid for was merely written on the cover. Later, proper handstamps were made with such inscriptions as POSTED UNPAID or MORE TO PAY, with perhaps the sum due as well. Often, however, the postman, to save time, did not bother to collect the postage that was due, and so in 1914 postmen were required to stick special postage due labels on these letters and call at houses to collect the postage that was owing. Each postman had to buy some of these labels from the Post Office as the Post Office thought that the postmen would try hard to get rid of them by sticking them on letters that were paid for incorrectly, and so claim the money themselves. Even so, some postmen seem not to bother about putting postage due labels on letters. Since 1914 when postage due labels were introduced, there have been labels at various times with values from a halfpenny to a pound, the higher values being used for bulky and overseas mail that is incorrectly paid for.

But stamps were not the only postal innovation of May 1840. There were others which, at first, Rowland Hill believed would be of far more importance than adhesive stamps. These were stamped covers and stamped envelopes. William Mulready submitted a design for the outside of the covers and envelopes showing Britannia bestowing the gift of cheap postage to the world, which pleased Hill but was unfavourably received by the public. Indeed, some newspapers criticised the adhesive stamps too – 'a little square bit of paper, about three-quarters of an inch long by half an inch broad, and as it chanced to be reversed when we first saw it, in the innocency of our hearts we mistook it for a patch of German corn-plaster. However, on turning it over, we saw it contained what purports to be the head of Her Majesty, very ill-executed.' These criticisms were in the minority, but the Mulready design was fated. Caricatures were of an openly rude description. Others attempted to advertise a cause (such as ocean penny postage or universal brotherhood) and both of these kinds of envelopes quickly appeared. As early as 12 May Hill wrote in his diary:

> I fear we shall be obliged to substitute some other stamp for that designed by Mulready, which is abused and ridiculed on all sides. If the current should continue to run so strongly against us, it would be unwise to waste our strength in swimming against it, and I am already turning my attentions to substitution of another stamp combining with it, as the public have shown their disregard and even distaste for beauty, some further economy in the production.

29 A letter sent from Halifax to London in April 1840. Adhesive stamps were not available until May. The letter was not pre-paid at the rate of a penny so it was charged double postage and marked with a 2d. handstamp. Postage due adhesives were not used in Britain until 1914.

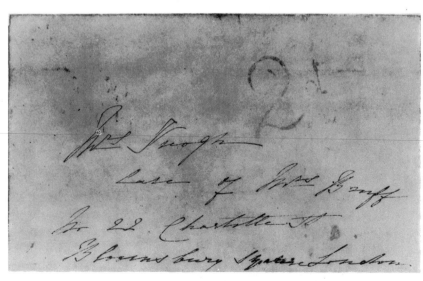

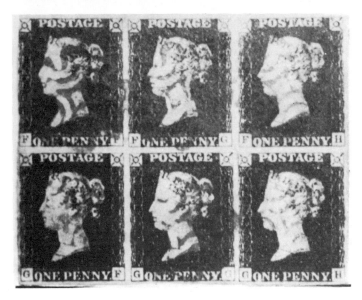

30 A block of six Penny Black forgeries. This was a clever kind of forgery made by photographing a sheet of stamps and using the actual photographic paper as stamps. These are known as forgeries in the second state, and are much more professional-looking than Penny Black forgeries in the first state, which are but crude imitations.

The Mulready envelopes were withdrawn early in 1841 and replaced by a stamped envelope, the 'Penny Pink', which had on it Wyon's embossed head of the Queen. Rowland Hill had been experimenting since June 1840 to see whether Wyon's embossed stamp could be printed rapidly and cheaply on envelopes and covers. Many of the Mulready envelopes were destroyed deliberately by the government. The Mulready letter sheets were sold until 1844, when they were replaced by embossed letter sheets. These show a marked similarity to the letter-cards and embossed envelopes which can still be bought in post offices today, for the cost of the stamp and a little extra for the cost of the paper. The early history of stamped stationery illustrates well the fickleness of the public and the fact that public taste and reaction cannot always be foretold accurately. Hill and the other reformers were quite convinced that of the two forms of pre-payment, stamps on the one hand, and postal stationery on the other, the latter would be of far more importance and would be accepted by the public more readily. At first, Hill devised the idea of adhesives mainly for the benefit of the illiterate. Many people, he believed, would wish to use stamped covers; stamps would be used by people posting letters already addressed by another hand. The reformers were wrong, and though postal stationery as well as stamps can still be bought at any post office the sale of stamps has always far outweighed the sale of stamped stationery. The public seem to have taken to the adhesive

31 A Penny Pink envelope introduced in 1841. The stamp, in pink, was embossed on the envelope before it was put on sale, in the same way that embossed postal stationery is sold today. These embossed stamps must not be confused with embossed *adhesives* which were issued at a later date.

stamps at once, as the following tale, recounted by Rowland Hill's daughter, suggests:

> To the post office of, at that time, tiny Ambleside, came one day a well-to-do man to buy a stamp to put on the letter he was about to post. 'Is this new reform going to last?' he asked the postmaster. 'Certainly,' was the reply; 'it is quite established.' 'Oh, well, then,' said the man, resolved to give the thing generous support, 'give me *three* stamps!' Not much of a story to tell, perhaps, but significant of the small amount of letter-writing which in pre-penny postage days went on even among those well-to-do people who were not lucky enough to enjoy the franking privilege.

1840 had been a busy and memorable year for the postal reformers. Their principal aims had been accomplished, but more required to be done yet. Certainly, Hill's scheme was a great success. This can be seen from the number of letters carried by the Post Office. In 1839 there were 75,907,572. In 1840 this number had increased to 168,768,344. Of course, all the names listed in this chapter deserve their share of praise for the changes that were introduced, but it is Rowland Hill who will remain always at the head of this list. The postal revolution was one of the most important changes introduced in the nineteenth century, one of the greatest social reforms of all. Henry Cole in his autobiography has left his estimate of the importance of the change he helped to bring about:

> All the progress of mankind is helped on by freedom of thought expressed in writing. The progress of religion, morals, health, science, education, arts, manufactures, commerce and international peace, are all advanced by correspondence which is next to nothing without the Post Office. It will be the glory of England for all time that she was the first country to adopt this ray of light, and the fame of Rowland Hill will be imperishable as having discovered uniform penny postage.

FURTHER READING
E. C. Smyth, *Life of Sir Rowland Hill*
A. James, *Sir Rowland Hill and the Post Office*

7 The Developing Postal Service

Though the principal aims of the postal reformers had been accomplished in 1840 – cheap uniform postage chargeable by the weight of the letter – in many senses the work of reorganising was just beginning. In the decades which followed, the plan was perfected to a very high degree. Rowland Hill and the officials in the Post Office watched out for forgeries and fraudulent re-use of stamps. Forgeries were attempted but they were few. The design of Victoria's profile and the intricate patterning round the head proved to be too difficult to emulate successfully. Fraud was a different matter. Many attempts were made to wash off the obliterating ink from postally used stamps so that they could be used again, and some of these attempts were quite successful. So many adhesives were partly cleaned and used again that a special postmark was made to stamp on the envelope when the Post Office noticed such a stamp. These postmarks were circular, containing the letters os (old stamp). Double postage was charged on such letters. The first kind of obliterating ink was red and the obliterating stamp was the so-called Maltese Cross. Quite soon, the colour of the ink was changed to black, as black ink was more difficult to remove than red, and, as it seemed rather pointless obliterating in black on a black stamp, the colour of the penny value was changed to red in January 1841. That was not the end of attempts to wash off obliterating inks, however, and it was many years before this problem was solved satisfactorily.

A great increase in the number of envelopes resulted from the postal changes of 1840. These, together with the stamped covers, were sold to the public un-gummed, though some dealers might gum their stocks before putting them on sale. The public in most cases had to gum their own envelopes or continue to use wax to seal their letters as before. The first person to suggest gumming all envelopes prior to sale seems to have been Captain Basil Hall, who wrote to Rowland Hill about his idea:

> It strikes me that a great convenience might be added to the envelopes if there were put a small lick of the gum which is used for the stamps at the angle where the wafer or wax is put; so that an envelope might be closed without the trouble of a wafer or the double 'toil and trouble' of a seal – implying lucifer-matches, tapers, and wax. I can easily see how one hundred, or any number of envelopes, might have this small touch of gum applied to them at the dash of a brush.

Hill's forecast that the number of letters would increase greatly was working out well, but the revenue suffered. In 1839 Post Office revenue had been £1,600,000.

In 1840 this fell to £500,000, and it was many years before the pre-1840 revenue level was reached again. Hill believed there to be several main reasons for the slow recovery of the revenue which could not have been taken into consideration in his original plan:

1   Delay in the adoption of stamps, and the still greater delay in effectually supplying the public therewith.

2   While my plan applied to inland postage only, large reductions were also made in foreign and colonial postage, which, however, right in themselves, of course had their effect in delaying the time when the amount of the gross revenue should have recovered itself.

3   The additional facilities to be afforded the public – more especially by a great extension of rural distribution – though a most important part of my plan, were, to say the least, for a long time delayed. This I conceive to be a main cause of delay in the recovery of the gross revenue.

4   Above all, the execution of my plan was, during the early years of penny postage, entrusted almost entirely to men whose official reputation was pledged, not to its success, but to its failure.

32   The back of a cover sent in September 1840 showing detail on the wax seal.

With a change in government, Hill was dismissed from office in 1842, but he returned as Secretary to the Postmaster General in 1846, and became Secretary to the Post Office – the job he had always coveted because it made him the permanent head of the Post Office – in 1854. Many of the postal successes achieved during this period were the result of Rowland Hill's industry and continual effort to see 'my plan', as he called it, prove successful. He never tired of talking about the Post Office and of asking foreigners about their own postal services:

The examined were of all ranks, from the King of the Belgians to Garibaldi, the Italian patriot, whom he met at a public banquet, and presently questioned as to the prospects of penny postage in Italy. Garibaldi's interest in the subject was but languid; the sword with him was evidently a more congenial weapon than the pen – or postage stamp. When, later, Rowland Hill told his eldest son of the unsatisfactory interview, the latter was greatly amused, and said: 'When you go to Heaven I foresee that you will stop at the gate to enquire of St Peter how many deliveries they have a day, and how the expense of postal communication between Heaven and the other place is defrayed.'

33 Not everyone used adhesives from May 1840. This letter of 1843 (notice that it is a folded sheet, not an envelope) is marked pd. (paid) by the sender in ink at the bottom left, and it has a hand-drawn 1 (penny) from top to bottom as well as a paid dated mark. Adhesive stamps were not made compulsory everywhere in Britain until 1853.

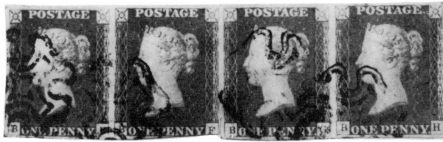

34 A strip of Penny Reds lettered in the lower corners BE, BF, BG, BH. By regulation each stamp had to be cancelled by an individual obliterating mark. The Two-Penny Blues have been torn from strips and not cut with scissors. A perforating machine was invented by Henry Archer in the 1850s.

Though Hill had the reputation of being a slave-driver and a man who was difficult to get on with, it is probable that no one else could have achieved what he did in such a short time, for he was striving constantly for the completion of his own plan on which he had spent the best part of his life's thought. He was knighted in 1860 and retired from the Post Office for health reasons in 1864. He died in 1879 and was buried in Westminster Abbey. Before his death, he saw many improvements introduced to the postal service, many of which he inaugurated himself.

Letters began to be carried by train in 1830, and the first travelling post office was established in 1838. The use of travelling post offices speeded up the flow of mail and the invention of mail-bag apparatus allowed letters to be thrown off a moving train and gathered into a train travelling at speed. In fact, the idea behind this apparatus was not entirely new, and neither was the idea of sorting mail during the journey. As early as 1826 Rowland Hill had thought it a useful idea to sort letters whilst the mail-coach was travelling. Nothing came of this idea, the partitioning of the interior of a mail-coach and the actual sorting operation being considered too difficult; but a primitive form of mail-bag apparatus was in use in the mail-coach era. When a mail-coach passed a post office it was not to stop at, the guard on the coach grasped hold of a handle or strap attached to the bag and pulled it aboard. Of course, the apparatus used for collecting and distributing mail-bags from moving trains was a refined art in comparison. The use of projecting arms and receiving nets effected the transfer, a system being used as early as 1838. Rowland Hill decided that the travelling post offices journeying away from London could deal with letters destined for

35 A mourning envelope with black edges, and an envelope handstamped with the numeral 813. Each important place had its own number, in this case the town of posting was Trowbridge (in Wiltshire) as can be seen from the circular postmark. Numeral obliterators were introduced in 1844 because the similarity of the Maltese Crosses made it impossible in many cases to tell where a letter had been posted; though, in fact, there were many different kinds of Crosses used, and some peculiar types could be pin-pointed to certain localities. From a complete list of numeral obliterators it was possible to tell where a letter had been postmarked, and at first circular named post towns were not included: see the mourning cover.

London from places nearby much more economically than direct sorting on trains travelling towards London, and would also save this mail arriving in London to be sorted there. So letters were sent on T.P.O.s travelling away from London on a night train, sorted, and then transferred to a train en route for London.

The London bellmen, of whom there were almost 100 at one time, disappeared in 1846. The bellman's locked bag with a slit through which letters were dropped gave way to the pillar-box, which both Rowland Hill and Anthony Trollope, the latter a Post Office surveyor, have claimed the honour of inventing. A pillar-box was erected in Jersey in 1852, though boxes had been used in France for several years previous to this. In London the first pillar-boxes were used in 1855 – 'It is proposed to fix boxes on the side of the footway, in such a position as not to obstruct traffic of any kind.' It was optional, of course, whether people posted their letters in pillar-boxes or took them to the post offices, as indeed it is today. Many people considered the latter far more secure. In one of his books, Trollope made one old lady, Miss Jemima Stanbury of Exeter, dislike:

> the iron pillar boxes which had been erected of late for the receipt of letters. . . . She had not the faintest belief that any letter put into one of them would ever reach its destination. She could not understand why people should not walk with their letters to a respectable post office instead of chucking them into an iron stump – as she called it – out in the middle of the street with nobody to look after it. Positive orders were given that no letters from her house should ever be put into the iron post.

The government encouraged and subsidised ships carrying mail, and not only for postal reasons. The enlarging of a merchant marine was a desirable factor from the viewpoint of political and commercial cohesion. The introduction of steam shipping led to a revolution in ocean transportation, and the sending of messages from one part of the world to another increased in speed. For example, when the *Great Western* was put on the transatlantic route in 1838 it took only $14\frac{1}{2}$ days to complete the journey. There was little uniformity in the rates of postage of letters sent abroad. From 1855 the average rate of postage on colonial letters was halved to about 6d. Letters to the West Indies cost one shilling, whilst those to Mauritius cost 10d. Letters to many foreign countries cost less than to the colonies; letters to many countries in Europe, for example, cost 3d., as did letters to the United States. Letters to Sweden and Russia cost 5d., those to Greece 8d.

The leader of the movement for low uniform postage on mail going overseas was Elihu Burritt, a lettered blacksmith from Connecticut. Burritt came to Britain in 1846 to agitate for cheap ocean postage. His plan for a League of Universal Brotherhood was allied closely to cheap ocean postage as a means of fostering communication and goodwill. It is of interest to note that Rowland

36 Travelling Post Office apparatus in use at Thirsk about 1900.

Hill was not in favour of this movement. He had his hands full enough trying to justify his financial prophecies outlined in *Post Office Reform* to speculate on such an unpredictable venture. Burritt and Hill both died in the same year (1879) yet before that year a uniform rate of cheap postage was set up under the provisions of the Universal Postal Union. Details of the U.P.U. will be outlined later in the present chapter.

The introduction of uniform penny postage for Britain in 1840 led to the creation of a new industry. Not only were postage stamps produced for the first time – in itself a tremendous undertaking – but the new system of charging by weight led to a boom in weighing machines. Envelopes began to be used extensively from 1840, and Christmas cards made their appearance after cheap postage was introduced. Henry Cole published the first Christmas card in 1843 and the shops quickly began to stock novelty boxes in which to keep stamps. Parcels had been carried by Dockwra's Penny Post in the seventeenth century, but the reforms of 1840, taking the view that letters were the Post Office's main concern, made no provision for their carriage; it was left in private hands. Rowland Hill persuaded the government that the value of a Book Post would be immense, especially in rural areas, and would help greatly towards the spreading of ideas. The Book Post began in 1848 at a rate of 6d. per pound, though at first the regulations were strict. Only one book could be wrapped in any one packet and writing was not allowed to be included – at first this meant that a book with the owner's name written inside was barred. The use to which the Book Post was put increased from 1855, when the rate of postage was lowered to four ounces for a penny.

The Post Office Savings Bank was opened in 1861, and this became an immediate success with the small saver. The P.O.S.B. is a good example of the many non-postal services which the Post Office has offered for over a century. The Post Office became the department of government which, more than any other, served the public directly in numerous related ways. The safety of money in transit was an important service that was instituted at an early date. The Money Order system was taken over by the government in 1840, and in 1862 the £5 limit on a Money Order was raised to £10. Soon many millions of orders were sent annually. For smaller amounts sent through the post, a postal note system (now called postal orders) began in 1881. They could be bought for amounts between a shilling and a pound, with poundage costing from a half-penny to 2d.

Though this book traces the story of the mails, it should be noted in passing that the Post Office has had the responsibility for developing telegraphic and telephone services. The world's first public telegraph was opened in London in 1839, and in 1866 a reliable cable was laid on the transatlantic route. Private companies ran the greater part of the telegraph service until 1868, when the Post Office took over all the inland telegraph systems. The telephone, too, had a rapid rise to fame. Graham Bell showed the value of his invention to Queen Victoria on the Isle of Wight in 1878, and almost at once a telephone service was established in Britain. The first telephone call to Paris was made in 1891. Since 1912 the Post Office has been responsible for almost all the telephone services in Britain. In 1958 H.M. The Queen dialled the first trunk call from Bristol to Edinburgh and introduced s.t.d. (Subscriber Trunk Dialling). From 1963 International Subscriber Dialling allowed subscribers in London to dial direct to Paris and other places abroad.

The Parcel Post began in 1883. This time Britain was not in the lead, as post

37 The first Christmas card (1843) designed by Henry Cole. It was about the size of a postcard. Such items as Christmas cards could be sent once postage was reduced to a penny an item in 1840. Instead of costing 1s. 3½d. for a letter from London to Aberdeen it only cost 1d.

offices in other countries began to carry parcels before this date, but the United States, where express delivery companies opposed a government parcel post, had to wait much longer (until 1912). In Britain the first parcel charges were 3d. for one pound in weight, up to one shilling for a seven-pound parcel, the maximum allowed at first. The Parcel Post did not really pay its way, for the railways charged 55 per cent of the postage collected on parcels for transporting them; and even though the letter-carriers already had heavy loads to contend with, it was necessary to burden them still further. By the end of the nineteenth century more than 67 million parcels were being carried each year. Naturally, the speed of letter-carriers was reduced, many of them leaving the post offices with parcels tied round their bodies, as well as carrying a heavy bag. Such things as umbrellas, bandboxes and fishing rods were given to the letter-carriers to deliver along with their ordinary delivery, and their bags often contained such things as:

> tin, wooden, and cardboard boxes, butter, Devonshire cream, fruit and flowers. And I have instances of game, partridges, rabbits, fish, and the whole of these have to be carried in the same bag with the letters.

Certainly, the letter-carriers found their lot vastly different due to the carriage of parcels, and for this reason their title was changed to postman in 1883. The high cost of sending parcels by rail led to a temporary reintroduction of mail-coaches on the roads in 1887. These were found to be so satisfactory – roads must have improved greatly since the early part of the century – that long-distance coaches left London for places as far afield as Manchester and Liverpool. After this temporary phase, horsedrawn vehicles of various kinds were used to carry mail for many years. There were horsedrawn parcel-coaches, mail-vans and mail-carts. Horsedrawn mail-vans were used last in 1949. Other forms of carrying mail locally were experimented with (especially after the introduction of parcel post in 1883) such as the 'hen and chickens', twin-driven cycles for parcel-post carriers, penny farthings, mail-baskets on tricycles, motor cycles with side baskets, bicycles, and, more recently, battery-driven delivery-vans controlled by

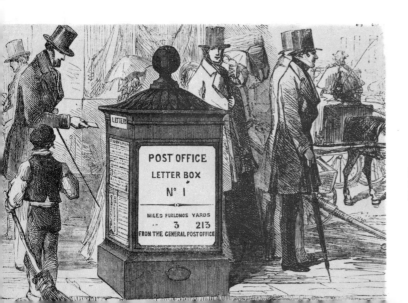

38 London's first pillar box (1855) situated at the junction of Fleet Street and Farringdon Street.

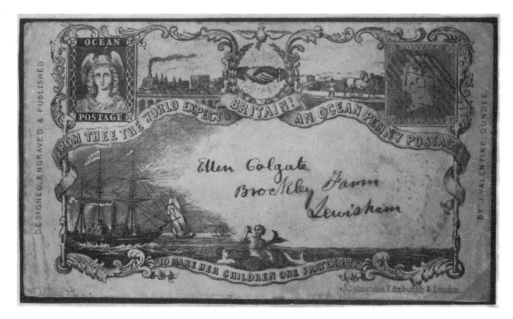

39 An envelope advertising the benefits of ocean penny postage.

a pedestrian postman. Motor vans began to be used to carry mail in the last years of the nineteenth century, and in the first decades of the twentieth century their use was greatly extended. The Post Office now has more than 16,000 red vans, ranging in size from mini-vans to articulated lorries for the road parcel services. Of course, railways are used still for the bulk of long-distance mail, but the value of the mail-van within smaller areas is tremendous.

Several other changes can be noted briefly. Postcards had been used first in Austria in 1869, and they were introduced to Britain the following year. The postage on postcards was a halfpenny. At first this charge was printed on the card before it was sold, but later it was allowed to stick an adhesive on postcards instead. The advent of commercial photography gave postcards such a boost that more than 200 million picture postcards were sent each year by the end of the century. Letter-cards were introduced into Britain in 1892. They were folded and sealed with the gum along the edges. They are still in use today, as are envelopes sold by the post office with the postage value already embossed on them.

With the increase in letter-writing in the latter part of the nineteenth century (in 1839 the average person sent three letters yearly, which had risen before the First World War to 66 per person in England and Wales, 50 per person in Scotland, and 35 in Ireland) went an improvement in street naming – in London at one time there were 60 'John Streets' – and also in house numberings. At least one case is known of someone moving house and taking the number of the house with her and installing it outside her new abode. She liked the number-plate and used it again even though it bore no relation to the numbers of the houses on either side! There were campaigns to encourage the public to put letter-boxes into their doors to facilitate delivery. One can assume the case of the Marquis of Londonderry to be exceptional. He wrote in anger to the Postmaster General asking if he was seriously expected 'to cut a slit in his mahogany door'. Many letters could not be delivered due to illegibility, partially incorrect addresses or to addresses being lacking totally. In one year, close on 31,000 letters were posted, all of them completely unaddressed, many of them containing money; and almost as hopeless were such letters confidently sent off bearing such addresses as 'My Uncle Jon in London'. It seems that it was well into the nineteenth century before the Post Office ceased to destroy letters it could not deliver from the information on the cover. Such letters were sent to the Dead Letter Office. Later, if the sender had written his own address inside, they were returned to him. This was the case until the Post Office Corporation took over from the G.P.O. It was decided towards the close of 1969 that the new Post Office, after a publicity campaign to encourage the public to address letters correctly, would destroy letters it could not deliver from looking at the outside of the envelope, either from the address on the front, or from the address of the sender which could be written outside on the flap of the envelope on the back. It was estimated that to cease to open and to return to their senders letters that could not be delivered would save more than a million pounds a year. Before such letters are

40 A pneumatic tube in use in London in 1863. The Post Office Railway (opened in 1927) was not the first attempt to get letters across London with all possible speed.

41 A Victorian pillar box in use at Framling-ham today. Notice the shape of the slit for letters.

destroyed they must be opened by post office officials to ensure that there is nothing valuable inside.

Letters sent to an address where the recipient no longer lived had been re-directed to a new address for an extra charge from 1840. If the new address was in the same town this charge was waived from 1855, but it was not until 1892 that the inland re-direction charge in Britain was abolished altogether.

The Universal Postal Union of 1875 co-ordinated earlier agreements between different nations with regard to responsibility for each other's mail, which it was agreed each member nation should carry as if it were its own. Much of the work involved in planning this union was that of the German postal reformer, Heinrich von Stephan. Twenty-two nations sent experts to the U.P.U. in Berne and a uniform rate of 2½d. (or 25 centimes) was agreed as the rate to be charged for letters of the lowest weight, up to half an ounce (or 15 grammes). Each country was allowed to fix a lower or a higher rate within certain limits. When letters were sent by sea over 300 miles an extra charge, not more than half the uniform rate, could be made. Other countries later applied for admission to the U.P.U., and this resulted inevitably in argument between member countries as to the

42 Some later Victorian stamps.

best way of including countries where long distances were involved. In 1875, for instance, Spain, Holland and France each wished to bring their colonies into the U.P.U., and Canada, Brazil, Newfoundland and India also wished to join. A uniform charge throughout the world was proposed by France, and Germany suggested that all countries outside the U.P.U. could be placed in four different groupings, each with its own rate. When such countries as India were admitted in 1876 an increased transit charge (double the uniform rate) on letters to far-off places was agreed to. An anomaly existed, however, for many of the letters sent from Britain to her colonies that were members of the U.P.U. paid rates of postage that were higher than the basic U.P.U. rate. Letters to India thus cost 5d., but if they were sent from France they went for $2\frac{1}{2}$d. It was not unknown for letters from Britain to her colonies to be carried privately across the English Channel and sent on to the colonies from the Continent at a cheaper rate than was possible from Britain. Largely due to the pressure exerted by an M.P. and ardent postal reformer, Henniker Heaton, who was a kind of latter-day Rowland Hill, the government agreed that postage on letters abroad should be reduced in 1891 to $2\frac{1}{2}$d. in those cases where it was higher. The fight for ocean penny postage was won completely in 1911.

U.P.U. congresses have been held over the years. The congress held at Washington in 1897 led to the international agreement which fixed the colours of the most commonly used stamps of each country for ease of identification – $\frac{1}{2}$d. green, 1d. red, $2\frac{1}{2}$d. blue. The U.P.U. is centred at Berne, and member countries send to Switzerland copies of postal notices and specimens of new stamps which are then distributed to other members.

43 A tricycle post began at Coventry in 1880. This photograph shows centrecycles in use at Horsham in the 1880s. These machines were nicknamed the 'hen and chickens'. The introduction of such contraptions was the result of the beginning of the Parcel Post in 1883. Soon ordinary bicycles were used as well as motor vans.

44 The development of postal uniforms. In 1792 the Secretary to the Post Office, who seemed to be against uniforms for letter carriers, wrote of the Postmaster-General's suggestion: 'The great good to be derived from the adoption of Your Lordship's ideas respecting the Letter Carriers, would be the prevention and detection of their loitering and mis-spending their time in ale houses or disorderly places.' The letter carriers in London were issued with uniforms in 1793, a scarlet coat with blue lapels and cuffs, a blue waistcoat and a beaver hat. In 1861 the scarlet uniforms were replaced by blue ones as these showed the dirt less. In 1868 the frock-coat was replaced by a tunic. In this photograph the men holding dates 1861 and 1868 should be labelled 'Letter Carrier' as the title was not changed to 'Postman' until 1883 when the Parcel Post was introduced.

Two interesting kinds of postal service have survived for some time – express services and registration. Private messengers were used in earlier times to send urgent messages. In 1891 a public express service began, costing 2d. for the first mile, 3d. for the second, and a shilling for every other mile. There are various express services today: a letter may be taken to its destination by a messenger from the Post Office; it may be delivered by a messenger when it reaches, in the ordinary way, the town of destination; or it may be sent Railex, which means that it is taken to the railway station by a messenger, and at the other end perhaps delivered by a special messenger. Of course, such services have to be paid for, and charges are not cheap, but they do exist for emergencies. Towards the end of the nineteenth century living things were allowed to be sent by express post, which resulted in the famous instance of two Suffragettes, having been refused permission to see Asquith, the Prime Minister, being posted to him express. They were taken to Downing Street and the police outside could not stop their arrival, for they were not allowed to interfere with postal articles in transmission. On arrival, however, they were not accepted at the door and so they had to be returned as dead letters to their sender!

Dockwra's seventeenth-century Penny Post in London included insurance on articles that were lost, and this was included in the single penny paid. Official registration of foreign letters started in the seventeenth century, though the charge was one guinea. Rowland Hill in *Post Office Reform* suggested a form of registration for inland letters and this began in 1841 when the charge was one shilling. Nowadays the registration fee for packets and parcels (and also letters) depends on the amount that is insured. High costs of registration have meant that many valuable letters once sent by registered mail now go recorded delivery instead.

The Post Office has been conscious of the need to improve speeds and to maintain services on schedule, and an impressive aid towards this end is the

45 The Post Office Railway carries sacks of letters under the streets of London, saving on surface speeds and on hold-ups caused by fog and traffic congestion. These containers filled with mail bags are loaded on the driverless trains.

Post Office Railway in London which runs underground from Paddington Station to the Eastern District Office in Whitechapel, six and a half miles away. There are seven stations along the route and the trains, which are driverless, travel at speeds of 35 m.p.h. along the tunnel, 70 feet below the streets of London. At the stations there are conveyor belts to take the mail-bags to the post offices above ground. The Post Office Railway was approved in 1913 but the First World War held up its opening until 1927. In the days when it was being planned, it was thought that the P.O.R. would greatly aid the rapid transit of letters across London, and it must be remembered that much of the traffic at that time was still horsedrawn and the congestion in London must have been hopeless. The P.O.R. beat the traffic problem and was not hindered by fog or other adverse weather conditions.

46 'Columbia' stamp-cancelling machinery made by the Columbia Postal Supply Company of New York. This electrically-driven machine could stamp 600 letters a minute and could accept bundles of faced letters from several facers at once, unlike earlier machines that were fed by one operator only. Britain bought 12 of these machines in 1902.

Letters were sent by air sporadically in early times by the use of pigeons and also by the use of balloons. Balloons were used to carry mail from Paris when it was besieged during the Franco-Prussian War in 1870. Letters were carried between London and Windsor in 1911 and were postmarked 'First United Kingdom Aerial Post'. A postal air service between London and Paris began in 1919, though the charge was half a crown an ounce. Flights in the 1920s were day flights with connections to trains that travelled by night. Gradually, air services were extended – London to India in 1929, London to Australia in 1934.

The sea route to Bombay took 14 days; this was cut to $2\frac{1}{2}$ days by air. Sydney was reached in 32 days by sea, and only 7 days by air. At first letters were carried by air between London and Windsor in 1911 and were postmarked 'First United Europe, under the 'all-up' service, went at the normal rate of $2\frac{1}{2}$d. if this provided the fastest means. Blue labels were issued to be stuck on letters sent by air, and from 1930 special blue pillar-boxes were erected for these letters. They were used only for a few years and were removed once letters began to be sent by air as a normal procedure. Private companies began internal air mail services in Britain which were not developed until well into the 1930s due to the efficiency of the night mails. Within the United Kingdom air transport is most useful when stretches of water have to be crossed. A service between Inverness and the Orkneys began in 1934. Letters to the Channel Islands and to Ireland are usually sent by air. In 1961 direct airmail services between Edinburgh and Belfast, and London and Glasgow were introduced. Air and shipping lines that carry mail are all commercial undertakings. The postal van has united the locality, the railway has united the country, and the shipping routes and airlines have brought together places across the world in a way that was not even dreamed of at the opening of the twentieth century. Letters can be sent to any continent in a matter of a day or so, and space is reserved for mail on almost all the fastest flights.

FURTHER READING
J. A. Mackay, *The Story of Great Britain and her Stamps*
R. Lowe, *The British Postage Stamp*

8 The Post Office and the Community

There are three important points to make in this last chapter: the value of mechanisation, the extent of the activities of any sub-post office, and the advent of the Post Office Corporation.

Approximately three-quarters of all postal costs are labour costs, so mechanisation is becoming increasingly important in order to cut down on such a high rate of expenditure. The revolution is taking place in the sorting offices, where it is not uncommon for a letter to have to be sorted three or four times before it reaches its destination. The automatic segregating machine is a large drum and as it revolves letters fall through hinged flaps to a conveyor belt. Packets stay inside and they are taken along another conveyor belt to have their stamps cancelled by hand. The letters are separated on a different part of the same machine, the wide envelopes being taken off by snatch rollers, the others being graded and stacked.

One of the trying jobs in unmechanised sorting offices is the task of facing. Thousands of letters are dumped on the facing table, and the facing staff have to pick up letters and turn them all round the correct way so that each pile has the stamps in the top right-hand corner. Piles of faced letters are sent on a moving belt to the end of the table, where they are picked off and taken to the stamp-cancelling machine to be obliterated. The job of manual facing was made more difficult when the two-tier postal charges were introduced in 1968. The widespread adoption of A.L.F. – the Automatic Letter Facer – does away with much of this work. This machine does three things: it turns the letters round so that the stamps are all facing the same way (which it does by means of detecting the phosphor lines on stamps); it separates first- and second-class mail; and it also cancels letters. A.L.F. can deal with 300 letters a minute. Automatic *sorting* is a complex matter and it hinges on the use by the public of post-codes when they address letters. By 1969 about half the addresses in the country had post-codes as the last line of the address. These codes are always in two parts, such as EH7 5AL, or NE10 OTQ. The first part of the code is the outgoing, the second part the incoming. In the code CRO 9LA, CRO means Croydon, and 9LA stands for the part of Croydon where the letter is to be delivered. Automatic sorting works like this. Letters that have passed through A.L.F. are sent to the operator of a coding desk, where the operator looks at the code on the envelope and types it on a keyboard. This prints two lines of phosphorescent dots on the envelope. One row of dots is below the address, one above. These dots, of course, express the code. Letters are then sent to letter-sorting machines where the first part of the code (the outgoing part) is read by the machine and the letters are sorted to 20 different

47 A sorting office is always a busy place, but particularly in the evening and in the early morning. Each sorter works with 48 pigeon holes which is the number he can reach without causing much stretching. Over the years improvements in the ordinary sorting offices have been introduced to make easier the moving about of large quantities of letters and parcels. Such improvements include the installation of lifts, chutes and conveyor systems. Large sorting offices, even of the traditional kind, are planned on the conveyor system, so that once mail enters an office it sets off along a set path, going from one section to the next, and this is designed to get the mail to despatch point as quickly as possible.

48 Postage stamps from the reigns of Edward VII, George V, Edward VIII, and George VI. All British definitive stamps have portraits facing left, unlike coins where the direction of the profile changes reign by reign. The last three stamps on the top row show Postage Due labels. The second stamp in the last row shows one of the Postal Centenary stamps of 1940 with the same profile of Victoria as used on the Penny Black and on all other stamps issued during Victoria's reign.

49 Heartbreak Corner in London showing what happens to parcels that are incorrectly packed. Many parcels never reach their destinations as the contents of badly-packed parcels are separated easily from their address on the covering paper.

boxes. This machine can sort 20,000 letters each hour. Other sorting machines further break down the destination of a letter; these machines sort to 144 boxes.

When letters reach their office of destination, the second part of the code (the incoming part) is read by other machines, and these sort the letters ready for delivery in that area. Several other countries are experimenting with automatic letter-sorting, but some of them take account only of the outward part of the code. In these cases, once letters reach the office of destination then manual sorting must begin.

Sorting offices of the future will be almost entirely automatic. Many of these are being planned at present, some already in use. Such a sorting office is rather like a continuous belt of operation, from the second that letters enter until they leave. Automatic machinery is so fast that a postman can take a load of mail to a sorting office, and then leave 20 minutes later with the same letters already sorted!

The extent of the activities in which the Post Office engages has become vast over the years. The days are long since gone when the job of a post office counter clerk was merely to sell stamps. A far from complete list of the services offered over a post office counter would include: stamps (postage, savings, and national insurance); licences (such as television, radio, dog, gun); road tax; stamped postcards; letter-cards; air letters; registered letters; recorded delivery; postal and money orders; national savings certificates; premium bonds; savings bank; and parcel acceptance. The Post Office pays out family allowances and old age pensions, and can thus be said to be concerned with life from birth to old age.

Perhaps it is rather unfortunate that one of the main grouses of the postman against the public (apart from illegibility) seems to be an insoluble one. Of

50 A.L.F., the Automatic Letter Facer, turns letters round the right way, separates first and second class mail, and then cancels it; A.L.F. can handle 300 letters a minute.

51 Post codes are transcribed on letters by a code operator so that they can be sorted mechanically. Perhaps in the future machines will be invented that can actually read the post code that the sender writes on the letter rather than the copy of the code that the operator transcribes on letters as at present. The problem of illegibility, however, is one that causes the Post Office many headaches.

52 A spacious post office. The new Westminster Bridge Road Branch Post Office. The circular shape of this post office affords extra space and pleasant working conditions.

53 The parcel section of the Mount Pleasant Sorting Office in London. Mechanical deflectors spread the parcels evenly to prevent pile-ups.

Britain's 97,000 postmen, more than 3,000 of them were bitten by dogs in 1968. Fingers are nipped at most commonly when letters are being put through letter-boxes. After the publication of these figures, the postmen's union wanted postmen to be allowed to carry dog-repellent sprays to protect themselves, but the G.P.O. rejected such a suggestion on the grounds that it might cause more trouble to the postman than it was worth; a postman could possibly be sued under the Protection of Animals Act of 1911. A suggestion that there should be a Protection of Postmen Act did not appear to gain much official support!

On 1 October 1969 the General Post Office changed its role and its name; it was no longer a government department, but a public corporation. The position of Postmaster General disappeared in the reorganisation, and was replaced by that of Minister of Posts and Telecommunications. The Minister has overall

54 The segregating table where letters are stacked into neat piles.

55 Mail is tipped on the conveyor belt as it arrives at the sorting office. Letters and packets are separated in the segregating drum.

56 Modern parcel sorting machinery.

57 High speed letter sorting machinery which can deal with 20,000 letters each hour.

58 Postmen leaving the office about to begin their rounds. Before setting off on a delivery each postman puts his own bundles of letters into his sack. This 'setting in' must be done in the opposite order from that in which the letters will be delivered. If a packet or a magazine roll is to be delivered, the postman reminds himself that there is such an item in his bag by turning upside-down or backwards the letter to be delivered at the house before the one the packet or roll is addressed to.

59 Elizabeth II stamps. *Top row:* Definitives. *Second row:* British regionals (left to right Wales, Scotland, Northern Ireland). There are other regionals for the Isle of Man. There were also regionals for the Channel Islands before these had their own Post Office from October 1969. England is the only part of the United Kingdom that does not have regional stamps. *Below:* special stamps to commemorate special events, anniversaries and British themes. Note that the third stamp in the third row has been partly shaded in this photograph because of the presence of the phosphor bands on the stamp which are there to allow mechanised sorting.

60 Printing stamps is a highly complex, specialised operation. After the sheets have been printed, they are perforated by a separate machine.

responsibility for the corporation, but the running of the organisation is in the care of the corporation's board. Postal workers ceased to be civil servants and became instead employees of one of Britain's nationalised industries. The task of the corporation will be twofold: to provide a good service at a low cost, but at a cost that pays its way. Thus, it has the difficult task of providing a public service and at the same time operating on a commercial principle. In its last year as a government department, the Post Office had a surplus revenue of £44 millions. In this respect the new nationalised industry began life on a healthier footing than many other nationalised industries. This is not to suggest that the new corporation will not have problems. In rural areas, for instance, the expenditure on collection and delivery exceeded income by £15 millions a year. Mechanisation or perhaps some modification of the services offered in rural areas might help, though the corporation must, of course, provide essential services. The same problem applies to the telegram service, if on a smaller scale, which lost £2½ millions in 1968. Fears that the Post Office may try to 'do a Beeching' would appear to be groundless, for the Act which set up the corporation states that it has a duty 'to exercise its powers as to meet the social, industrial and commercial needs of the British Isles'.

Indeed, it cannot be assumed that the Post Office will be able to increase postal charges very readily when faced by difficulties. During the first Christmas of the two-tier postal charges, 11 per cent fewer letters and cards were sent than in the previous year. This shows that the cost of sending messages, perhaps surprisingly, is price-sensitive to some considerable degree. It would seem that shortages of money in the corporation as a whole will have to be met by increasing telephone charges.

The Post Office is the most important single employer of labour in the country,

61 The new type of pillar box with the square look makes the job of emptying boxes much easier, for the sack is hooked under the internal metal frame inside the box where the letters are lying, a lever is pulled and the hinged bottom drops away letting the letters fall into the sack. This reduces the chances of letters being damaged in wet weather. Such boxes can be supplied in units or in pairs as shown here.

62 Trolleys have been used experimentally at almost 50 offices in Britain. The trolleys are lightweight and are designed to effect faster delivery in the streets and to make easier the job of carrying heavy loads.

with 400,000 workers. These include administrators, power and electrical engineers, architects, medical officers, solicitors, typists, clerks, postmen, sorting clerks, counter officials, telephonists, telegraphers, messengers, Post Office Railway workers, wireless station operators and cable ship crews. The Post Office sets out as a commercial operation, and the years ahead will see many changes. Certainly, the challenge of new ideas and techniques will make the service offered to the public faster and more reliable than ever before.

FURTHER READING
Philatelic Bulletin, monthly
Post Office: Report and Accounts, annually

Chronology

1516	Sir Brian Tuke appointed Master of the Posts
	Routes for the King's Mail established on the main roads from London
1632	Thomas Witherings appointed Master of Posts for Foreign Parts
1635	Witherings reorganises the inland postal system
1661	Henry Bishop introduces postmarks
1680	William Dockwra begins a Penny Post in London
1720	Ralph Allen organises the cross- and by-posts
1760	The Crown's right to revenue from Post Office receipts commuted for a sum in the Civil List
1784	John Palmer begins the mail-coach service
1801	The London Penny Post turned into a Twopenny Post
1830	First mail carried by rail, between Liverpool and Manchester
1837	Rowland Hill's *Post Office Reform*
1838	Travelling Post Office set up between London and Birmingham
1839	4d. uniform rate from 5 December 1839 to 9 January 1840
1840	Uniform penny postage from 10 January for all $\frac{1}{2}$-oz. letters
	Franking abolished
	Adhesive stamps and Mulreadys sold in May
1841	Penny Black changed to Penny Red
	Envelopes with embossed stamps used instead of Mulreadys
1846	Last year of London mail-coaches and of London bellmen
1847	A shilling adhesive for foreign post
1852	Pillar-box installed in the Channel Islands
1861	Post Office Savings Bank
1870	$\frac{1}{2}$d. postcards
1875	Universal Postal Union
1881	Postal orders
1883	Inland Parcel Post
1891	Rail letters and express service
1896	Motor vans used to carry mail
1897	Penny postage for letters up to 4 oz.
1898	Imperial Penny Postage
1909	Post Office distributes old age pensions
1911	George v Coronation air mail, London to Windsor
1918	Minimum letter rate 1$\frac{1}{2}$d.
1919	Transatlantic airmails from Newfoundland
	London to Paris airmail

1924	Britain's first commemorative stamps
1925	First airmail to South Africa, Sir Alan Cobham
1927	Post Office Railway opened in London
1929	Imperial Airways service to India
1939	Letters for India, South Africa and Australia carried by airmail at ordinary postage charge
1940	Centenary of Penny Postage
	Letter rate increased to $2\frac{1}{2}$d.
1942	Airgraphs allowing photographic microcopies of letters
1956	Premium Bonds
1957	Postal rate 3d.
1965	Postal rate 4d.
1968	First class minimum 5d., second class minimum 4d.
1969	General Post Office becomes a public corporation
	Minister of Posts and Telecommunications replaces Postmaster General

Index

The numerals in **bold type** refer to the figure numbers of the illustrations.